Refounding America:
A Field Manual for Patriot Activists

Terry Easton
Ashton Ellis

Welcome to the Second American Revolution

For Classical Liberals, Conservatives & Libertarians
For Republicans, Independents & Real Democrats
It's about the Individual versus the State, not Right-versus-Left

Liberty Publishing Company LLC

LPC

Refounding America: A Field Manual for Patriot Activists

First Edition published July 4, 2010

Cover and design by Erica Simone (*www.ericasimone.com*) and set in Minion Pro and Bell Gothic Std types.

Printed and bound in the United States of America

Library of Congress Control Number: 2010907354

Easton, Terry & Ellis, Ashton

Refounding America: A Field Manual for Patriotic Activists
by Terry Easton & Ashton Ellis
-1st ed.
p. cm.

ISBN-13: 978-0-9749694-4-2 (paperback: alk. paper)
ISBN-10: 0-9749694-4-3 (paperback: alk. paper)

1. Title [1. Political Science - Essays 2. Economics – Essays.]

FIRST PRINTING
Liberty Publishing Company LLC
www.libertypublishingcompany.com

The book website is: www.refoundingamericabook.com

E-mail addresses:
General inquiries: info@refoundingamericabook.com
Media contact: media@refoundingamericabook.com
Quantity & group purchase: groups@refoundingamericabook.com

What the Media and the Experts Say
About Refounding America:

•**John Fund, *Wall Street Journal*** Columnist. Author of *Stealing Elections*: *How Voter Fraud Threatens Our Democracy*

"One of the most dramatic developments of the last year has been the re-birth in people's interest in the Constitution, the Founding Fathers and the first principles of liberty.

Refounding America is a compelling effort to put the animating beliefs that began America into today's context of soaring debt, bloated budgets, rampant nationalism of whole sectors of the economy and weakening of our currency. It's a book that is a one-stop-shopping guidebook for how the people can reclaim the destiny of America!" (see: *opinionjournal.com*)

•**Lee Rodgers, *ABC Radio*** Long-time #1 Talk-Radio Host:

"This is a book for those who have decided, however reluctantly, that we have arrived at an "us vs. them" juncture in American history. Listening to the "bring us together" braying of both Republicans and Democrats has had one con-sistent result – giving in to so-called "progressivism." Easton and Ellis make clear that only an in-your-face response holds any hope for the salvation of the America that was once but is steadily fading into an inconsequential status under the pow-er-mad promoters of unlimited government control." (see: *RadioRodgers.com*)

•**Jerome Corsi, *World Net Daily*** Reporter. Author of *The Obama Nation*:

"***Refounding America*** is a handbook every 21st Century American Patriot needs to read to know the key issues and tactics involved in preserving, protecting and defending the Constitution of the United States." (see: *WorldNetDaily.com*)

• **Dinesh D'Souza, *Author of Multiple New York Times #1 Bestsellers***. Author of *The Enemy at Home*:

"***Refounding America*** is a field manual for American patriots. It not only provides a critique of the progressive nostrums of today's politics; it also shows the way out of the morass and how citizens can organize effectively to restore the American dream. Read it--and get moving." (see: *DineshDsouza.com*)

•**Ken Schoolland, *International Society for Liberty*** President. Author of *The Adventures of Johnathan Gullible*:

"Dynamite! This book is pure, intellectual dynamite! Easton & Ellis have written an exquisite patriot field manual more complete, more compelling, and more timely for the defense of liberty than Thomas Paine's Common Sense. It is a call-to-arms for the brain! It is boot camp for every citizen who feels that Washington, D.C. is poisoning the life spirit of America.

Do they stir fear and hatred? No! Easton & Ellis muster reason, compassion and courage. They demonstrate that the statist arguments can be dissolved with logic and humor. Easton & Ellis have a superb grasp of what riles the statists and of what comprises their weakness.

Refounding America is written with extraordinary clarity, with masterful organization and wit. After laying out the foundation for a free society, they show the whole arsenal of tools for winning it back. It is not only to be read by every liberty-loving American. This book is to be lived if we are to have liberty at all." (see: *ISIL.org*)

•Alex Deane, *BigBrotherWatch* Director:

"For years, Terry Easton's columns in *Human Events* have analyzed and explained the global economic landscape with wisdom and accuracy. Few have better explained the need for liberty and fiscal responsibility with such consistent clarity. Now, with exquisite timing, he and Ashton Ellis have produced a remarkable guide to campaigning and thinking that deserves to be read by anyone who cares about the future of freedom. My organization has benefited from *Refounding America* – and so can yours!" (see: *bigbrotherwatch.org.uk*)

•Dr. Eamonn Butler, *The Adam Smith Institute* Executive Director. Author of *The Best Book on the Market: How to stop worrying and love the free economy*:

"*Refounding America* is a breathtaking book – much more than a mere list of concerns about the way America is going and a restatement of America's values. It's also a practical manual on how ordinary Americans can actually get their tool kit together, get under the hood, and set about fixing things." (see: *AdamSmith.org*)

•Morton Blackwell, *The Leadership Institute*:

"Millions of highly motivated, newly activated conservatives and classical liberals now realize they owe it to their philosophy to study how to win. Just in time for their arrival into politics, *Refounding America* is the field manual they should use to achieve victory!" (see: *LeadershipInstitute.org*)

•Ron Robinson, *The Young America's Foundation* President:

"*Refounding America* is the "how to" book for the American Patriot who is fighting the battle to unwind the tentacles of creeping progressivism and big-brother statism in Washington and state capitals throughout the land. If you love the Constitution and the great American values of free enterprise, liberty, personal freedom and the right to run your own life without a Nanny State telling you what to think and how to live, then this book is for you. It is a call-to-arms to take back America and restore the values of our forefathers. Buy this book now!" (see: *YAF.org*)

CONTENTS

Foreward

This book is about values, principles, honor and integrity, sorely missing in America's political elite today. It is about loving your neighbor as yourself - even if they sometimes get confused and lose their moral compasses in this hectic and complex society.

This book is about peacefully changing the federal and state governments throughout America to restore those values, and to throw out the Progressives and Marxists who have infiltrated the Democrat and Republican parties.

If you are someone who loves the US Constitution and freedom, and the inalienable Rights of the individual which are given by God, not the State, then welcome aboard.

If you are a life-long Democrat who has watched the soul of your proud old party founded by Thomas Jefferson ripped out and replaced by a godless Marxist shell, then here you can find some help to restore your party.

If you are a life-long Republican who has watched the conservative message of helping the individual and family by encouraging entrepreneurship, independence, pride & personal responsibility replaced by the mushy "feel good" pabulum put out by the old guard politicians, then this book will be a breath of fresh air.

If you are an Independent fed up with both "Twiddle Dee" and "Twiddle Dum" parties, then we're with you. It's time to toss all the corrupt rascals out of office, especially the ones who give lip service to the phrase "we the people" - by which they really mean "we, your elite masters".

If you hear church sermons on "social justice" misusing both words to mean Marxist stealing from one group to "give" to another, destroying the morality of charity in the process, then amen, brother. Charity means voluntary giving by each person, not government stealing. Charity is moral. Theft is sinful. Jesus didn't say "let's have the government do it", he said "you do it". From the bottom up, not the top down.

Calling something a "democracy" doesn't make it moral. When two wolves and a sheep have a "democratic vote" on what's for dinner, the result is not moral. Morality comes from God & one's own heart, not a government dictator or "democratic" rulers. The sadistic killers Stalin and Hitler used to rant on and on about their "glorious democracies" - totalitarian dictatorships which systematically murdered over 50 million people who got in their way. Thank God that America was founded as a Republic, not a Democracy.

We have a lot to cover. Keep Gandhi and Martin Luther King in your mind always. Remember Jesus said: "Love your neighbor as yourself". Gentleness and kindness will be the way that we will win against Satan's work and his twisted & diseased offspring, the hateful "isms:" Progressivism, Marxism, Communism and Fascism.

We are on the side of truth and love and freedom and humility. We are fighting against lies, hate, slavery and power-mad psychotic narcissists - the former anarchists of the 60's who have transformed themselves into the government whose twisted dreams of a Marxist dystopia have never been closer to happening.

This book was written to give you the tools to win against this nightmare. And our companion site: *www.RefoundingAmericaBook.com* has lots more too.

The authors:

Terry Easton & Ashton Ellis

July 4, 2010

Introduction

"There is but one straight course,
and that is to seek truth and pursue it steadily."

-George Washington

Welcome to the Second American Revolution!

Welcome to 2010.

You are reading this book because you have a deep and sinking feeling in the pit of your stomach that the America you have grown up in, and loved and cherished over the years, has been mortally wounded and is dying.

You are a conservative or libertarian. You are a Republican, Independent, or Democrat who was inspired by John F. Kennedy. You are a "classical liberal" who treasures the system of government that the Founding Fathers created, designed to protect our unalienable natural rights of "life, liberty & the pursuit of happiness" from a dictatorial government.

You are angry because you feel that your country is being stolen right in front of your eyes by downright evil or just plain stupid people who have been dazzled by the false god of Progressivism nee Marxism. You can see that a corrupt Marxist rump of the proud Democratic Party has hijacked the machinery of that once-glorious party to do its bidding.

And the goal of this current batch of power-mad politicians and unelected Apparatchik and Czars is to turn us into obedient serfs by stealing our money and snuffing out our liberty.

Moreover, the current batch of bumbling Republican politicians seem to have lost their values and their noble party's heritage too. Do they support the Constitution and the Bill of Rights or not?

The countdown for your future has begun. The book that you now hold in your hand can save your life - and your country. It is time to *Refound America*!

1776 was 10 generations ago. It's up to our generation to restore to America the basic values of our Founders so that there will still be a bright future for the generations to follow over the next 234 years.

Our side stands for truth, for goodness, for love, for the little guy, for the underdog, for the consumer, for the mothers and fathers and children of America. The other side stands for darkness, for corruption, for evil, for their naked grabs for power, for your slavery, for raw Marxism.

We are fighting a war for our very freedoms.

It's not a question of Left versus Right. These are old-fashioned labels that date back to before the French Revolution[1]. They referred to where the parties sat in the King's chamber. They were all still subservient to the despot king.

These labels are used by the two-headed political beast of Washington politics to confuse us. Don't buy into them. Freedom-lovers measure the scale from bottom to top, not left-to-right. It's you, the individual at the bottom versus the Big Brother state at the top. And Big Brother's boot is getting bigger every day.

So the test for freedom and liberty is simple: Citizen versus The State. Support for the little man, the common Citizen versus toady or naive follower of the power hungry Washington-New York "Axis of the Elites".

It's not too late to turn back – although it's nearly so!

We're at 5 minutes before midnight, and the clock is ticking…

Glenn Beck, our modern Paul Revere has been sounding the alarm for many months now. The time to stand up and take action is now.

If an individual politician works to increase your personal freedoms and liberties, if she works to protect your natural rights from the State's all-powerful grasp, then we will support them for election. If he works to crush the Bill of Rights, to continue to promote the Big Brother - Big Nanny all-powerful State with control over ever aspect of your life and property, then we are against him.

On Tuesday, November 2nd, 2010, we will have perhaps the final chance to bring America back home to a more moral, wiser, and financially sound country. We MUST NOT lose this opportunity. It may be the only chance we have in our lifetimes to save ourselves, our children, and our fellow Americans.

As Americans, it is not only our birthright, but our *duty* to protect our God-blessed country and those fundamental truths our Founders fought and died for.

This is more than "Life, Liberty and the Pursuit of Happiness" and the Bill of Rights.

This is more than our right to keep the money we earn and the property we own, to have the right to freedom of expression and worship, and the right to bear arms, the right to privacy, and to simply be left alone.

The rot has become too deep.

We are in danger of having our country stolen away from us under our very noses, just as happened to the democratic, freedom-loving, but Depression-crushed German people in the 1930's. It only took a single crisis (the burning of the Reichstag in 1933) and two laws under Adolf Hitler, the Reichstag Fire Decree[2] and the infamous Enabling Act[3], to extinguish Democracy and usher in Totalitarianism.

In the United States, the framework of progressive Statism - and its corrupt love affair between big government and big business – also began construction under the Great Depression. Politicians on both sides of the aisle were enamored with European Fascism and Soviet Communism[4].

After World War II, Statism retrenched a bit. But by 1961, Republican President Dwight Eisenhower warned Americans[5] about the growing dangers of the "military-industrial complex". He cautioned that "the destructive rise of misplaced power exists and will persist."

Statism resurfaced big time after 9/11[6] under the Bush Administration, and continues to grow at breath-taking speeds under the Obama Administration[7]. Fortunately, the new machinery of total government control is still under construction. It won't be completed until the end of 2010.

One more crisis, perhaps another major terrorist attack which, this time, kills millions of Americans, may be all it takes to implement draconian repressive laws. Then, "lawful" but obscure and semi-secret Presidential Executive Orders (already on the books[8]) can suspend our fragile civil liberties and complete the transformation of our country into a one-man dictatorship.

We are fighting a battle for our lives, a battle against the forces of oppression that are corrupting the soul of our nation.

Progressives follow a simple formula in making citizens addicted to an ever-expanding government: they promise benefits to one group while taxing another. The "rich" lose money, but the "poor" lose as well; they lose their freedom to choose and become dependent on the State for their housing, food and education. Eventually, there are no more "rich" or "poor" people; just heavily taxed citizens modifying their behavior to get a bigger piece of a dwindling, government-controlled pie. The end result is an entire nation whose soul is lost through small, avoidable corruptions.

For ourselves, our children, and the rest of the world we have only a few months left to stand up in public and make a difference.

You have bought this book just in time! Your authors deeply thank you for your bravery. We will be there with you step-by-step on our united journey to *Refound America.*

Lets Get Started!

This book is a "How-To" handbook for you, the American Patriot.

In it, we give you the tools and show you the ways that you can personally use to *take back America.* It will be fun, it will be liberating - but it will also be hard work. For there is a war going on in the United States today. It is a war for your freedom. And we cannot afford to lose.

You must become a community activist.

You must *immediately* get involved with other like-minded friends and neighbors. You must go public and make a fuss, even a big fuss. You must do things that you, a quiet, hard-working person, busy with your own life, family and career would never think of doing – much less giving enormous amounts of your time. In the process, though, you will become more peaceful with as your focus and clarity grows. You will become closer to your family as your values sharpen and your anger is transformed into positive force.

You will learn how to capture the media's attention, to focus your thoughts into bullet points, to provide sound bites and photo ops to the press just like the slick Progressives do who are right now waging a war against your freedom.

You will learn how to shoot down any Progressive you meet - and know when not to waste your time arguing with them. We give you the ammunition to win independent voters and true freedom-lovers over to your side.

You won't have to take your life in your hands as our Founding Fathers did. But you may be verbally harassed by some of the wackos who will feel threatened by your actions. But you will be able to laugh at them, to see them as the buffoons that they really are. And what a joy it is to make fun of our enemies. Nothing so destroys a pompous, arrogant and stupid opponent as a bit of ridicule.

So here's Secret #1: the Progressives can't handle being made fun of. Their skins are so thin and they are so self-righteous, ridicule destroys their fragile egos. Since emotion guides their thinking, common sense humor flusters them.

See, now wasn't that fun to think about? Thought so! That's why we've filled this book with funny cartoons and illustrations to make our point. We hope you laugh a lot as you ponder the ideas inside.   It is our responsibility to help empower you. And if we do the job right, you will join with us to help save this precious country of ours.

Once you finish ripping through this book, there is a special web site with tons more pages of goodies, strategies, contacts, links, and other stuff – that's "for your eyes only". On the last page of this book is printed a "secret code", an ID access code unique to this book. It's your private password to our extensive private website: *www.RefoundingAmericaBook. com.* Use it to access the site. After you create your own unique ID, it will work for you and you alone. You can download items, link up with fellow Patriots, and use the powerful web-based Internet tools to reach out to legislators, the media, and other friendly groups.

What's in the Book?
Here's a quick summary of just what you'll find inside *Refounding America.*

Part I. The Core Principles of Freedom:
If you do nothing else, share this section with everyone you know. Especially your spouse and your children.

Building a philosophy of life is like erecting a tall skyscraper. We first have to dig down to the bedrock of core beliefs before we can lay the cornerstone of our moral society. This is the point where the Socialists fail. Their moral system - as they see it - is, in fact, based on faulty logic. It's mostly just a jumble of confused emotions. Unlike their name implies, Socialists do not build real societies at all. They try to erect a mythical 'Utopia', a place where everyone is equal because the government makes them so. It's little wonder that every time they start construction, the entire dream turns into a grotesque nightmare full of high taxes, suffocating regulations, and enforced leveling.

But there is light to fight this darkness. "Ye shall know the truth," says Jesus, "and the truth shall set you free[9]."

In Part I, we cover step-by-step the core principles that have made this country and our society the greatest and freest and richest that has ever existed in the world. And we do it in a way that makes it very easy to share them in a few words with others.

Throughout the book, we'll be talking a lot about how to think in sound bites and mind images as you actively reach out to the media and your neighbors. And no arguing is necessary; just calm, occasionally humorous explanations.

Just as a math teacher doesn't have to argue that 2+2=4 or an economist that you can't spend more than you take in and not go bankrupt, we have the real world of truth on our side. And with a bit of wit and a great deal of warmth and kindness, we'll win the confused and lost souls back home.

Part II. The Current Issues:

Ever wanted to have the facts at your disposal to shoot down a Progressive blathering on about some crisis of the day? Or better yet, to be able to reach the media with forceful one-liners and quips that make them laugh by showing up the absurdity of the other side's wacky beliefs?

In this section of the book, we present you with 15 current issues as argued about in the media today. Each chapter is divided into two perspectives: Progressives and Classical Liberals. Progressives are for more government, more control for them, and less freedom for everyone else. Classical liberals oppose Progressivism in all its forms, and advocate for free markets, free choices, and free associations. While other ideologies fall somewhere between, these two schools of thought provide the clearest, simplest philosophies on government.

And yet, the average Progressive doesn't want to be ruled by a Police State, to be watched night and day by Big Brother, and to be coddled by a Nanny State that has an iron fist inside a not-so-soft glove. Really, they don't.

The secret here is to talk with Progressives about common human values. You don't share any with them? Sure you do. We all do.

We all want to do what we want to do when we want to do it! The desire for personal freedom: to travel, to have your own money to spend, to not have the government spying on your every move - these are common human values.

Democrats are big on civil liberties, and they should be. The drip-by-drip loss of our civil liberties, for the Progressive and the Conservative alike, is a common ground we share. We can unite on these issues alone. And once we get a Progressive to say, "you know, I agree with you on that", we've started the process of making a friend and bringing them back in from the cold. Remember, they are afraid of us. We shouldn't be afraid of them.

In Part II of this book, we go through the 15 "Big Issues" with a gentle hand and a bit of humor. Honey always works better than vinegar. (Yes, your mother was right). Most loud-mouth Progressives are angry and afraid. They desperately need some honey.

Part III. The Basics:
In this section we jump right in, roll up our sleeves and talk strategy with you.

Who is the enemy"? How well do we know them? What is their real motivation? What are their secret goals? Do we understand their dreams - and their fears? Then we explore who we really are and what we really want ourselves. To know thyself is critical to putting your thoughts into action. And action by millions of Americans is what's needed in today's war of ideas.

We then turn to the nitty-gritty details of how to build a community of interest and join up with other Patriots to *Refound America*. The end result is a collection of strategies, techniques and tools that will show you how to take back America.

Let's pause for a moment to thank the Progressive guru, Saul Alinsky. In his classic text on community organizing, <u>Rules for Radicals</u>, he identifies the key methods for picking targets, building coalitions, and pressuring the powers that be into meeting demands. Not only does the book provide an insight into the mind and strategies of Progressives like Barack Obama, it takes pains to relate Alinsky's principles in the most objective way possible. The result is a how-to manual that can be used by any person or group! So we follow David Horowitz's master strategy: flip the paradigm upside down & throw them off balance by "Inverting the Myth[10]"! It's simple. It's fun. And it works.

And what's the myth? That the Progressives care for the underdog: women, children, minorities, and the poor. This is the Big Lie.

We show dozens of examples of how the Progressives intentionally make permanent victims of the people they pretend to help. And then we move on to show how to make fun of their failures and spotlight their corrupt policies. You'll find immediate tools to help kill off current Socialist plans like "Government-Run Health Care" and "Global Warming". It's been over 45 years since the great "War on Poverty" was kicked off by President Lyndon Johnson - along with hundreds of billions of wasted taxpayer dollars, and still we have not yet won the "war".

Why? For the same reason that State-run schools are dumbing down America's kids: Progressives think a small group of people – "experts" – have all the answers, and should be allowed to force-feed their decisions on everyone else. That's how we get one-size-fits-all, "comprehensive" solutions from Washington, D.C. for our health care, taxes, public schools, energy, even food! If it were in the real interest of the political elites to promote human flourishing, they would be returning power to the local levels of society - where policies can be made by the people most directly affected by them.

Part IV. The Tool Box:
Here's where we pull out all the stops. Now that you're fully charged and ready to go, you'll need a set of tools to make it happen. Want to get a local interview with your newspaper? We've got some tricks and techniques to use. Want to get big coverage from your local TV station - who will then send along their footage to the network news pool? We'll tell you how to do it. Want to multiply your efforts by thousands rather than knocking on your neighbor's doors one-by-one? Use the Internet. We'll give you the short-cut answers on what to do, where to do it, how to do it and when.

This chapter gives you the meat-and-potatoes menu of the Patriot Activist. After you read it, you will feel a lot closer in spirit to Paul Revere - but equipped with the instant communications tools of the 21st century.

Part V. The Resources:
There's still a bit more to cover. Where can you turn for help? With whom should you network? What organizations can you plug into? Which news outlets are the movers and shakers - for the Progressives as well as Classical Liberals? What are the really important books out there that you can read to shore up your knowledge about liberty and the power of freedom?

Part V, our collection of Resources, links you to the world. You are not alone. There are literally tens of millions of other Americans who feel exactly the way that you do, who believe the things that you believe, who share your values. The Resources section of this book has perhaps the most important function of all: to connect you with our private web site which, in turn, is loaded with lots more ideas, strategies, and supports that you can load into your own personal arsenal of "weapons of truth". There is an iceberg of resources waiting for you to tap into just below the surface. This book is just the tip which juts above the water. The rest is waiting for you.

It's okay to be angry, so long as you channel it towards fixing the problem. Use this book to convert your anger and frustration into action and power. Empower yourself to be that community activist for patriotism!

A Special Note for Our Hesitant Democrat Friends:

Please join us! We need your help to take back America!

This book is written for the Classical Liberal, the freedom-loving citizen that shares the convictions of the Founding Fathers who gave birth to America. The Founding Fathers held certain truths to be self-evident. They saw our rights of life, liberty and the pursuit of happiness as "natural rights", given by God, not the State. Our rights were enshrined in the Bill of Rights, that precious document that protects each citizen and sovereign state, against an all-powerful Federal Government.

There's a chance you may really be a Classical Liberal - and not even know it.

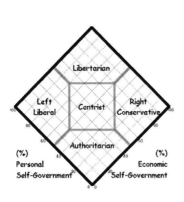

Check out the simple test for liberty at *www.theadvocates.org* to see how you score for freedom. Over 14 million fellow Americans of all political persuasions have taken this test so far. See where you fit on the chart below. You'll probably be surprised.

Do you believe that our government has a right to read your e-mail, wiretap your computer without court order, or tell you how to behave in the privacy of your own bedroom? Does the government have the right to prevent you from smoking tobacco or marijuana "for your own good"?

Does the State have the right to "regulate" the Internet and the media to control what you can watch or read? Do you have the right to keep most of the money you earn over your lifetime? After all, the only thing you ultimately "own" is your time. Or does the State have the right to take up to 70% of your earnings away from you to spend it as its political elites sees fit, pocketing 30% of your taxes for bureaucratic overhead?

Do you believe that government is part of the problem, or part of the solution? Are you afraid of the government and its power, or, as the Founding Fathers believed, should the government always be afraid of you, its citizen? What does "we the people" really mean?

Are you proud of Washington politics today?   Or are you ashamed of how corrupt Big Business, Big Lobbyists, Big Unions and wealthy politicians have been turning Washington into a form of Corporatism[11], run by the multimillionaire elite who pay lip service to the little people?

Both of the major political parties treat the public treasury like a personal piggy bank. Henry Paulson, a billionaire, was the head of Goldman Sachs. He left to become George W. Bush's Treasury Secretary, orchestrating the first bail-out of Wall Street. Obama's Treasury Secretary, Timothy Geithner, bailed out bankrupt insurance giant AIG in his role as former head of the New York Fed Bank. He continues the bailouts in his new job.

The biggest winner? Goldman Sachs got $13 Billion in initial AIG payouts alone[12]. Meanwhile we US citizens are stuck with a bill, so far, of between $200 to $250 billion to bail out AIG - so that Wall Street banks won't suffer. That's more than the Afghanistan war cost in total over the past 10 years to date. Goldman Sachs was Obama's biggest Wall Street contributor. They paid his campaign $994,795[13] . Not a bad return on investment for them - 1,300 times.

Surprised?

Obama promised over eight times[14] during his presidential campaign to hold all legislation meetings on C-Span in the public's eye. Instead, the Democratic members of Congress and the White House are now holding secret meetings behind closed doors. All elected Republicans and all the press are locked out, while the Progressives hash out massively unpopular and unwanted laws, against the wishes of the majority of the population, according to current polls from multiple news organizations[15].

Are you aware that most of the billionaires in the United States today are registered Democrats whose fortunes pull the strings of Washington politicians - on both sides of the aisle[16]? Did you know that most Wall Street bosses, like hedge-fund master George Soros, are also registered Democrats who use the party to carve out special interest deals and tax breaks for themselves? Check out the statistics at the Federal Election Commission (*www.fec.gov*[17]) and *Guidestar.org*.

Did you know that for the past 40 years the vast majority of registered Republicans come from the middle class ? The Republican Party today looks like the classic 'bell-shaped" curve of American families. The Democrats, on the other hand, now represent a "double-humped Camel": a large class of wealthy people on the right-hand side of the curve and a smaller group of poorer families on the left-hand side - with a noticeable depression in the middle.

So, is this battle being shaped as a class-warfare struggle - the middle class[18] versus the poorer families - with the wealthy mostly Democratic elites safely above it all and pulling the strings?

Over the last 100 years, corrupt politicians aided by sincere social "collectivist" activists - both Socialists and Fascists - came to form an unholy alliance of so-called "Progressives". Although they preached a peaceful Utopia free from fear and want, their methods and tactics of bringing it about were brutal in action. By the late 1930's, they had even captured the name "Liberal" away from the true Classical Liberals who built America on the rule of law and equal justice for all. Progressives began to systematically use 'Liberal" and "Progressive" and "Democrat" interchangeably. And it worked.

True Classical Liberals are people who believe in the equality of people, who abolished slavery, who won the vote for women, who fought for civil rights, who eliminated the draft[19].

Classical Liberals were renamed "Conservatives" and "Libertarians" by the Progressives, just as the Progressives got Peter Jennings and ABC Nightly News to flip the colors of the election day party maps from red to blue. By doing so, the long-standing Democratic color proudly shown - red - was replaced by royal blue on the TV maps. Why? So that the party could separate itself from the Red Chinese and Red Soviet colors of the communist flag.

Did you know that the Republican Party was founded by Abraham Lincoln who paid for the abolition of slavery with his life? Martin Luther King was also a Republican. The Civil Rights Act of 1956 was passed by Dwight Eisenhower, the Republican President who was the Supreme Allied Commander who won World War II against the Nazis. It was President Gerald Ford, a Republican, who abolished the draft on January 23, 1976.

By the mid-1970's the Progressives began to eat into the heart[20] of the proud old Democrat Party as of John F. Kennedy and Bobby Kennedy. By the end of the 1990's, they had captured its soul. Fine old Classical Liberal Democrats like Henry "Scoop" Jackson from Washington and Daniel Patrick Moynihan from New York were gone.

It's been a tragic loss. The real Democrats have been replaced by people like Rep. William Jefferson of Louisiana, who was sent to prison after the FBI caught him[21] with $90,000 of cold cash stashed away in his kitchen freezer, part of $½ million he pocketed in bribes and payoffs.

Read up on the proud history of the Democratic Party and its hero's of the past 200 years.

Thomas Jefferson founded the Democratic Party in 1792 as a congressional caucus to fight for the Bill of Rights and against the elitist Federalist Party. In 1798, the "party of the common man[22] " was officially named the Democratic-Republican Party and in 1800 elected Jefferson as the first Democratic President of the United States.

Oh, the irony! Jefferson fought for the individual natural rights of the citizen against the all-powerful State. He fought for everything that is the *exact opposite* of the Progressives.

We need your help to fix the Democratic Party! Don't let it collapse into a morally-bankrupt shadow of its former glorious self. The party of Thomas Jefferson needs your help.

America needs competition inside its parties and between its parties. The free marketplace of ideas is vital to civil discourse. The battle needs to be about freedom and more freedom, not State control and more State control. Remember: "a government big enough to give you everything you want is a government big enough to take from you everything you have[23]."

One size fits all, one master State, one official opinion, only one voice allowed are ideas that true Democrats abhor. Although the Progressives who have seized control of the Democratic Party are systematically crushing all dissent within the party and expelling members and politicians who disagree with them[24], we need you stand up and fight for justice and open debate within your party, not secrecy and deal-making held behind smoke-free-mandated doors.

Do you remember September 12th, 2001? It was the day after 9/11. Strangers hugged each other throughout the land. American flags flew everywhere. The world stood by us in support. And we were all proud to be Americans. We were one nation, under God. It's time to reunite our country in the spirit of liberty and freedom and compassion that we've always shown.

Join us - and lets *Refound America* together!

TIP: *www.RefoundingAmericaBook.com* is our Internet website loaded with information which links into each Book Part and Chapter. Also, a special Insider section is open only to readers of this book. That includes you! Later on we'll provide you the secret information on how to access this private, closed section of our web site. In the meanwhile, whenever you see this computer icon next to the text, it's your tip to look at the website for lots more stuff.

[1] http://en.wikipedia.org/wiki/Right-wing_politics

[2] http://en.wikipedia.org/wiki/Reichstag_Fire_Decree

[3] http://en.wikipedia.org/wiki/Enabling_act

[4] Liberal Fascism, by Jonah Goldberg, 2007, Doubleday, New York

[5] http://www.h-net.org/~hst306/documents/indust.html

[6] http://www.cato-at-liberty.org/2010/04/12/bush-was-a-statist-not-a-conservative

[7] http://www.realclearpolitics.com/articles/2009/08/23/a_doctrine_of_no_re-treat_98005.html

[8] http://www.archives.gov/federal-register/codification/executive-or der/12148.html
http://akadad.bizland.com/rps/fema.htm

[9] http://scripturetext.com/john/8-32.htm

[10] http://newsrealblog.wordpress.com/2009/11/24/david-horowitzs-advice-to-the-tea-party-movement

[11] http://www.washingtonexaminer.com/opinion/blogs/beltway-confidential/Free-mar-ket-populism-Ron-Paul-says-Obamas-not-socialist-hes-corporatist-90538989.html

[12] http://www.reuters.com/article/idUSN1548789520090316

[13] http://www.opensecrets.org/pres08/contrib.php?cycle=2008&cid=N00009638

[14] http://www.breitbart.tv/the-c-span-lie-did-obama-really-promise-televised-health-care-negotiations

[15] http://www.realclearpolitics.com/epolls/other/obama_and_democrats_health_care_plan-1130.html

[16] http://www.fatcatdemocrats.com

[17] http://www.fec.gov/finance/disclosure/disclosure_data_search.shtml

[18] http://answers.yahoo.com/question/index?qid=20080711071054AA7vrib

[19] http://en.wikipedia.org/wiki/Classical_liberalism

[20] http://www.prospect.org/cs/articles?article=a_liberal_shock_doctrine

[21] http://www.nola.com/news/index.ssf/2009/08/william_jefferson_verdict_guil.html

[22] http://www.democrats.org/a/party/history.html

[23] http://www.phrases.org.uk/bulletin_board/60/messages/53.html

[24] http://www.politicususa.com/en/Frank-Kick-Out-Dems

PART I: CORE PRINCIPLES OF FREEDOM

Part I covers the Core Principles of Freedom. These principles are necessary to create good, just, and ennobling laws that maximize the freedom of every individual. If we are going to re-found America, our fellow citizens must re-learn those self-evident truths about the Laws of Nature and nature's God.

We believe that freedom - for the individual - is the best means for securing peace. Respect for an individual's life and property are essential requirements for creating a just society. Over the course of seven chapters we discuss these and other ideas behind our nation's founding, and their continuing importance to secure the blessings of liberty and our continued individual and mutual prosperity.

Chapter 1 introduces the Two Fundamental Laws of Life. The first is "do all you have agreed to do." The second is "do not encroach upon another person or their property." The health of civil society hangs on these two principles.

Chapter 2 digs deeper into the Second Fundamental Law, and uncovers the relationship between private property rights and personal freedom. From the moment of creation, every person enjoys four basic property rights[1] over their own life, ideas, possessions, and the legal documents that recognize them.

Of course, not everyone agrees. Progressives and Marxists violate these fundamental rights through theft masquerading as redistributed taxes. They see all rights as applying to groups, not individuals, and subject to government control and whim, not God-given and inalienable.

Chapter 3 shifts the focus towards the misguided idea of "collective rights," especially as claimed by governments. But institutions don't have rights – only people do. The idea goes even deeper. It is the individual person alone – not groups of individuals like government – that can experience both freedom and accountability. The government cannot have legitimate power when it cannot be punished. The government can have duties, but it can never have rights.

Chapter 4 centers on our Constitution's clearly stated purpose to create a limited federal government of 30 or so enumerated powers, such as the power to establish a post office. It is important to remember the Tenth Amendment. It reserves all the unmentioned powers in the Constitution to the States or to the people. Our national government is charged with doing only those things that the several states cannot easily do alone, such as raise a common army or settle interstate trade disputes.

Chapter 5 details the Bill of Rights. The Bill of Rights was created to protect the people from an out-of-control government. The government, of course, doesn't need protection from the people; it is a creation of the people. The first eight bills guarantee specific rights to each American citizen, while the last two bills reserve all the rights and powers to the people and the States that are not expressly given to the federal government. A common-sense reading of our Constitution and Bill of Rights establishes a federal government much smaller than the bloated one we have today. The Founders did not intend a pervasive, duplicative regulatory system with state and federal laws suffocating citizens. Rather, they wanted the power of each level of government to reflect its proximity to the people it serves. They wanted power to flow from the bottom up.

Chapter 6 defines commonly used, but usually misunderstood terms like Government, the State, Capitalism, Socialism, Communism, Fascism, Corporatism, and Progressivism, among others. We need to know what these terms mean and the differences between them so that it becomes easy to spot a policy or argument that moves America closer to a totalitarian state. Progressives love to misuse words intentionally. Like 'Democracy'. In the USSR, Stalin loved to call his dictatorship a "democracy" of the people[2]. Rubbish.

Chapter 7 briefly sets the stage for the importance of "Austrian Economics" as the clearest, simplest, and truest explanation of economic behavior. It shows how the present love affair with Keynesian Economics (just print all the money you want) is false, but useful to corrupt politicians. With its shared understanding of the human person, Austrian Economics is the soul mate to the Constitution. A more detailed discussion of Austrian thought is found in the first four chapters of Part II.

Chapter 1

The Two Fundamental Laws of Life

"Liberty is the source of prosperity"
- Richard Maybury

A model is the way we construct our internal understanding of how the world works. It is our belief system that grounds our spiritual center. It provides us with a sort of "Universal Truth" that we live by, and expect others to live by as well.

We are fortunate. We grew up in America. Tens of millions of our ancestors left dozens of other countries to come to America as individuals and families, one-by-one. In many cases, they landed with nothing much more than the shirt on their back and, if they were lucky, a few gold coins in their pockets.

Why did they come? What were they seeking?

They came in search of liberty and personal freedom. They came in search of religious freedom. They came in search of fortune and the right to own property. They came in search of happiness. They came with the hope and the dream that if not for themselves immediately, than at least for their children, there would be a better life, a life free from corruption and kings, wars and religious persecution. Perhaps a life to start their own business, or perhaps a life to just be left alone.

Our American model of universal truth is enshrined in the Declaration of Independence, which states up front: "We hold these Truths to be self-evident, that all Men are created equal, that they are endowed by their Creator with certain unalienable Rights, that among these are Life, Liberty, and the Pursuit of Happiness". This is a revolutionary document. Never before were such words so boldly written.

Our Founding Fathers believed that one's happiness was the highest right that we could aspire to obtain.

Over the centuries many models from various philosophers proposed to explain how "the world works". Many were written for kings and dictators to justify their raw power over their subjects. Some were written by utopian theorists who dreamed of imaginary worlds where real people don't live.

As with many theories, most models proved false for several reasons:

1) they violate the underlying "laws of nature"; that is they are contrary to how things actually work or are physically programmed to work, either by the laws of physics or our DNA coding, and

2) they failed when put into "real world" practice and tested.

But a few survived because of their universal truth. The United States uses the two fundamental principles of the old British common law as the legal model for our Constitution.

These are:

(1) Do Everything that you agree to do

(2) Do not encroach upon another person or their property.

The first principle is the basis of contract law. The second is the basis of tort law and some criminal law[3].

These are the two laws taught by most religions and philosophies, which is why they were the basis of *common* law - the law common to all. They form the basis of the American model of universal truth. When these two fundamental laws are not widely obeyed, the only options are tyranny or chaos because oaths can't be trusted, and boundaries aren't respected.

Travel throughout the world. You will see that countries in which these laws are most closely obeyed by the people and their governments are the ones with the most liberty, prosperity and peace. Their citizens are genuinely happy. Those countries which ignore these laws are dominated by totalitarian dictators. They are desperately poor, paranoid places whose ordinary citizens suffer short, brutish, desolate lives[4].

Richard Maybury is the Publisher of the Early Warning Report, which tracks the battle between the free world and "Chaostan" as he calls it. (see: www:chaostan.com). He refers to the two fundamental laws as the basis of his understanding of 5000 years of world history.

He has also written a wonderful collection of books in his "Uncle Eric" series that are great for sharing among adults and students alike. You can order the set from our website *RefoundingAmericaBook.com*.

Mr. Maybury has been studying the application and effects of the two fundamental laws his entire life:

"These laws are essential for an advanced society. The first gives rise to trade and specialization of labor. The second creates peace, security and goodwill. Many animals are social. Wolves, ants, chimpanzees and whales come to mind. Each social species has laws for social conduct coded into their DNA. These laws exist to promote the well being of the species.

When a member of a wolf pack violates a law, he is punished by other members of the pack. If violation of the rules is widespread, the whole pack is punished by nature. The pack ceases to operate harmoniously, food becomes difficult to acquire and members die. Humans have more free will than other species and therefore more ability for individuals to violate laws, but the laws are there, in our DNA. These laws are higher than any human law, and human law cannot repeal them.

When these laws are violated, the result is some kind of damage to someone. Good intentions do not prevent this damage, nor do euphemisms. When stealing is called a tax, it remains stealing and it is every bit as damaging. Widespread violation of the laws by anyone, including a government, causes damage until the civilization collapses and the survivors, if any, must start over, as in Europe's Dark Ages."[5]

Key Concepts:

The Two Fundamental Laws:

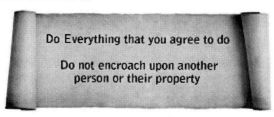

Do Everything that you agree to do

Do not encroach upon another person or their property

Quote:

"A democracy can only exist until a majority of voters discover that they can vote themselves largesse from the public treasury."

-Historian Alexander Fraser Tyler

Slogans & Bumper Stickers Idea:

WE'RE A REPUBLIC SIR! NOT A DEMOCRACY!

Chapter 2

Property Rights and Personal Freedom

"Morality stems from Property & Property Rights, and the clear separation between 'Mine' and 'Yours'".

The second fundamental law talks about property: "Do not encroach upon another person or their property".

Strange as it may seem to some, property and its ownership is the fundamental basis for all personal freedoms. Without the right to own property, there can be no freedom, only slavery.

Most living creatures are extremely acquisitive and territorial. Deer fight battles for territory. A female won't mate with a male who has no territory. The male must be "rich" in territory or she can't raise her family.

Human beings share this same hard-coded DNA to own "property" (a form of "territory"). Even among children raised in the Israeli socialist Kibbutz or the experimental youth camps of the USSR, one of the first words that children learn is "mine".

Acknowledging this innate natural law of property, governments create laws to recognize the existence of property and to establish a set of just rules to protect the ownership of property. This includes its creation, transfer, use and destruction. Property can also be shared between two parties who agree in how to share it. For example, a landlord might rent his property to a tenant, and a software programmer might license his property to a user.

Very quickly, as a person grows up, he comes to understand that there are various forms of property, and they form a hierarchy of sorts.

"Primordial" property that an individual possesses is given to each of us by our Creator. It is our own body. This is the highest property right. Only you own your life. As an adult, you are responsible for your own actions. While your parents brought you into this world and raised you as a child, upon reaching adulthood, your life is yours to do with as only you please. You can squander it or treasure it. You can even end it. But it is your property only. This is what the founders meant when they wrote: "We hold these truths to be self-evident...", that men "...are endowed by their Creator with certain unalienable Rights, that among these are *Life*...".

It's really quite simple. In a moral or just society, no one has the right to own another person. Slavery is illegal. In a just society, the State does not have a right to own your life either. Thus, there can be no conscription, no forced draft to serve the King or dictator or government. To be just, such service must be voluntary.[6]

When a person owns his own life, he naturally owns the ideas of his own mind. For example, a person can envision building a log cabin in the woods. He can see the trees cut down in his mind, vision the logs being laid together, and living in the home with his family. Given a bit of time, and a bit of strength, he can clear an acre of land and in a few months his mental vision will become a physical reality.

The vision of a log cabin is a new form of property. This is the primary property of your ideas, the fruit of your mental thoughts.

As before, a just society recognizes these rights too. We call them "intellectual property rights". People are creative beings. We talk and sing and draw and dance and invent machines. Modern intellectual property rights therefore take various forms: copyright to protect our writings, patents to protect our inventions, trademarks to protect our unique identities, and trade secrets and processes to protect our more complex creations.

But what about the real log cabin itself?

The actual log cabin is a form of secondary property. These are physical things that you can build with your brawn and your tools, using the natural resources available at hand. The original log cabin can catch on fire and burn down, but the vision of the log cabin in the builder's mind hasn't been destroyed. Given enough time, a new, even better log cabin can rise up from the ashes.

So, secondary property is a form of property that comes into existence from our primary property, the ideas of our brains. A just society recognizes ownership of secondary property such as real estate (land and buildings), machinery and human constructions or other physical artifacts like cars, TV sets and books.

Lastly, there is a third and final form of property, tertiary property.

Perhaps you and your brother work together to build houses for your two families. It turns out that you are really good at it. A neighboring farmer asks you to build one for him, in return for a life supply of fresh milk. And soon another neighbor swaps some chickens for a house. And so it goes down the years. You and your brother's reputations have grown throughout the land and your home construction services are always in demand. Eventually, you want to retire and pass the business on to your only son. Your brother wants to do the same with his two children. So you two draw up an agreement of sorts, a contract that passes your rights to own your business to the next generation.

A just society recognizes these property rights as well. Forms of partnership interests, corporation shares, bonds and IOU's, and other abstract financial instruments are written into laws that respect and protect the owners of these properties. And this new tertiary property is also being invented all the time. This means that new wealth is being created all the time too.

Think about Google. It is a fabulously wealthy company. But what does it do? It provides a support service to expand the powers of your mind, a form of mental tool that didn't even exist a decade ago. Google has made millions of shareholder-owners wealthy. And the gross domestic product of the United States has grown tremendously through the creation of similar new companies like Yahoo, Microsoft, Amazon, and E-Bay.

Remember, property rights flow downward from our Creator through each individual and onward. And in this way, they form the basis of basic morality: the relationship between God and man, and the relationship between one man and another.

For ten thousand years of human existence, both philosophers and ordinary folk have recognized the natural order of property and its rights. The old Mesopotamia tablets dug up at the gates of Babylon show property contracts between buyers and sellers. These anticipate the truths taught by the nomadic tribes of wandering Jews and the Bible by thousands of years.

Over time an entire body of corporate law has emerged which deals with the recognition of all three forms of property, which might have originally been created many decades or even hundreds of years ago.   The oldest corporate organization on the Earth has had its property protected by successive waves of civil governments for almost 2,000 years. It's called the Roman Catholic Church.

Let's do a short mind experiment.

Suppose that there was only one person living in the world. Would there be a need for property? Like the unborn baby in the womb, this sole person would assume "it's all mine". More likely, since "you" and "yours" wouldn't exist, such a thought wouldn't even arise.

Yet once we are born into a world with but one more person in it, a clear and moral separation of "mine" and "yours" is the only way to define relations between you and me. The toddler first learns this playing with others in the sandbox. My "right" to punch you in the nose stops at the tip of your nose. Most wars have been fought over this problem of property rights. "What I want, I take", say's the dictator. Of course, we all learned the Golden Rule as a child: "Do unto others as you would have them do unto you".

Some people still get confused about all of this.

Some people think that they have the "right" to take your property and give it to someone else. Most people would call this stealing. Progressives call it "redistribution". It sounds better.

Perhaps Marxists and Progressives never learned to understand the difference between "mine" and "yours" when they were growing up. Bullies and mass murderers often suffer from the same problem. Psychiatrists tell us that a psychopathic killer has no moral problem "taking the life" of another person, because to him, that person has no right, primordial or otherwise, to his own life. It's really that simple.

What Marxists and Progressives refuse to see is that freedom is greatest when a society has a strong sense of property rights. When property rights are weak, especially when the government justifies the arbitrary use of force of its guns to take an individual's property away, freedom is lost. The immoral ability of the King to steal the property of the colonists was eloquently written down in the Declaration of Independence, and is the basis on which a rag-tag group of Patriots fought a war against England, the most powerful empire on Earth at that time. In other words, the battle for our freedoms was fought over our property rights.

Read the Declaration of Independence: The King had *"plundered our Seas, ravaged our Coasts, burnt our Towns, and destroyed the Lives of our People"*. Line-after-line talks about the theft of people's property: *"He has constrained our fellow Citizens taken Captive on the high Seas to bear Arms against their Country"*. The King has cut off *"our Trade with all Parts of the World"* and imposed *"Taxes on us without our Consent"*. He has *"sent hither Swarms of Officers to harrass our People, and eat out their Substance"*.

DONT TREAD ON ME

Powerful stuff. No wonder, one of the oldest Revolutionary flags, known as the Gadsden Flag, was a snake inscribed below with the words *"Don't Tread on Me!"*.

Laws that protect property between individuals are well developed in the United States of America. However when the government itself wants to take a citizen's property, the laws have been immorally *"reinterpreted"* over the years to allow the government to seize a person's individual property. Recent rulings from Progressive Judges in Connecticut and New York[7] say it's now constitutional for your local town to seize your house and turn it over to a rich out-of-town property developer, using the rubric of "*collective good*".

It was not always so. To the Founders it was obvious that property was the basis of all freedoms. In fact, the Declaration of Colonial Rights drawn up by the First Continental Congress on October 14, 1774 to list grievances against the King, identified the people's inalienable rights as "life, liberty and property".

By the Second Continental Congress, Thomas Jefferson had rewritten and expanded these grievances into an impassioned plea for freedom and the right "to the pursuit of happiness". These revolutionary words were finally adapted and approved in a closed session on Tuesday, July 2nd, and released to the people on Thursday, July 4, 1776.

Key Concepts:

➤ Primordial Property (your life)   Primary Property (your ideas from your mind)   Secondary Property (your physical possessions)   Tertiary Property (your stocks & bonds)

➤ Because new property is continually being invented, wealth is continually being expanded.

Quotes:

"*Private property was the original source of freedom. Is still is its main bulwark.*" -Walter Lippman

"*The reason why men enter into society is the preservation of their property.*" -John Locke

Slogans & Bumper Sticker Idea:

> **You can have my property when you pry it from my cold, dead fingers.**

Chapter 3

The Individual's Rights versus the Government's "Rights"

All freedom starts with *you*. You are the sovereign over one person: yourself. Our lives are gifts from God, not the State. Our *fundamental rights* are, therefore, inalienable because no one can justly take them away from you or me (unless we, of course, have forfeited a fundamental right by, say, killing another individual). This includes kings and dictators, slave-owners and governments. When each of us voluntarily joins with other like-minded individuals to form a group of people, that group does not magically acquire any more "rights" above those that each and every individual member of the group already possesses.

In particular, the right of the majority to force the other members of the group to obey their collective will is not a moral or legitimate right. It's pretty obvious when you think about it. If two wolves and a sheep come together and vote *democratically* on what's for dinner, the outcome of that vote is pretty obvious. And the sheep won't be happy! Violent groups of people have a well-known name when they act as a single collective. We call them a "mob".

All groups of people coming together in common cause are formed voluntarily by each individual acting independently - with only one exception. Where you work, what church you attend, what sports club you might belong to, which town you live in, these are all groups of people with whom you have voluntarily associated.

However, there are some things that most people feel they cannot do by themselves or in free association with others.

Two basic problems quickly surface: 1) How do we defend our joint interests (our homes, fields, and factories) from invading armies and dictators from outside our borders? For this most people agree we need a government. 2) How do we jointly protect ourselves from the crooks and thugs among us who would do us harm? This second problem deals with establishing a "rule of law" and a judicial system. Many people think that the government should do much more than that, for the *general welfare* of *the people* as a collective, but therein lies a big problem.

A government is the only group of people to which we individually give the unique power to rule over our actions. Government is the single institution that has the power to use "legal violence" over its member-citizens, whether an individual agrees or disagrees. And woe to him who disagrees! Resist and you risk losing everything, including your life. Let's hope that you are not a sheep who has found yourself surrounded by a pack of wolves!

You cannot voluntarily withdraw from the power of this collective group of people unless you physically move away to be under the jurisdiction and protection of another government somewhere else. And the Earth has become quite a tiny planet over the past 200 years. Dictators understand the power of the government all too well. Mass-murderer Mao Zedong said it clearly in his Little Red Book[8]: "Power comes from the barrel of a gun". As Dictator-in-Chief of Communist Red China, he practiced that maxim by murdering well over 60 million people.

Though it provides the greatest amount of popular participation, there is nothing to prevent a "dictatorship of the democracy" from arising and following the false cries of a charismatic "savior" such as Adolph Hitler in Nazi Germany. *Der Fuhreur* was originally elected through a democratic vote, and with the permission of the majority of the people he transformed Germany into a fascist dictatorship. Anticipating such abuses, the Framers of the US Constitution established a republic with checks-and-balances on the people as well as the political elites.

By the way, there is another institution of people which we recognize that uses illegal violence over the people under its control. We call that the mob or mafia.

Since we give the government such awesome powers over us, it should be obvious to anyone that we would surely want to limit the reach of responsibility and authority that any government can enforce. We want to limit its scope with the same understanding that the English historian and moralist Lord Acton wrote in a letter to Bishop Mandell Creighton in 1887: *"Power tends to corrupt, and absolute power corrupts absolutely. Great men are almost always bad men."*

It's necessary to remember: Governments don't have rights; only people do. Governments have duties. To carry them out, we the people delegate some of our powers to them. Thus, government is an invention of the people. The people are not slaves to the Government. The people create government and the people can replace it, redesign it, or abolish it at their will.

Governments habitually go bad as they grow in power and size. They have been compared to cancers in the body politic, always wanting to grow bigger and more powerful. So, the best government tends to be the most limited in its scope. Not necessarily the weakest; just the most limited.

Our Founding Fathers created the Constitution of the United States with this concern in mind. They knew what they didn't want. They didn't want the new government to grow so big and powerful that they would become afraid of it.

The funny thing is that even the most radical Progressives don't want government, any government, telling them what to do. Yet Progressives like using the force of the government to tell you what to do. When they take power, they often exempt themselves from the rules that they apply to other people. Kind of like Congress.

Key Concepts:

> Your Rights are Inalienable. They are given to you by God, not the State.

> The Government has no rights of its own.

Quote:

"You have rights antecedent to all earthly governments; rights that cannot be repealed or restrained by human laws; rights derived from the Great Legislator of the universe." -John Adams

Slogan & Bumper Sticker Idea:

You can't change the government until you change the people in the government.

Chapter 4

The Constitution: You, Your State and the Federal Government

Since we know that power always corrupts, the Founders designed the United States Constitution to do three things:

1) Cripple the power of the Federal Government by keeping it small and starving it of money. For example, federal income tax was unconstitutional for America's first 140 years. The tiny central government's duties were restricted. Most power resided closest to the people, with their governor and state legislature. Then came the 16th Amendment.

2) Prevent any one person or group from staging a coup and seizing control of the Federal Government by installing a set of checks and balances at every level of government. For example, there are two houses of law-makers; three equal and independent branches of government: the Presidency, Congress, and the Court.

3) Define and codify a Bill of Rights to protect citizens from the police power of the Federal Government which could be used against them, and to limit Washington's powers to only those described within the four corners of the written Constitution document. The Bill of Rights was written to protect the people from the Federal Government, not the other way around.

In doing so, the American Founders intentionally created a *republic*. They did *not* want a *democracy*, because they knew that raw, unchecked democracy quickly degenerates into a tyranny of the majority. Alexander Hamilton wrote, "We are now forming a republican form of government. Real liberty is not found in the *extremes of democracy*...If we incline too much to democracy, we shall soon shoot into a monarchy, or some other form of dictatorship".

The Constitution therefore states, "The United States shall guarantee to every State in this Union a *Republican* Form of Government..." This establishes the foundation for a Federal Government of limited power whose principal obligation is to protect the rights and liberties of the people. This charter of power granted to the government from the people was not intended to be changed easily. It was not to be a "living document," subject to the passing fads of future eras. Instead, it was – and is – a collection of first principles.

Now is a good time to thumb through the Constitution. It's a beautiful document designed to safeguard our rights from enemies foreign and domestic.

If you don't have a copy of the Constitution handy, you can down load one from our book website: RefoundingAmericaBook.com. We'll also send you a free, bound pocket copy of the Declaration of Independence and Constitution when you log into the Insider section of our website. More details on this free private section open only to our book readers will be provided later on in this book.

The Constitution gives the Federal Government very specific and limited duties. Roughly 30 enumerated powers are listed, most of which are clearly spelled out in Article I (the Legislature), Article II (the Executive) and Article III (the Judiciary).

Specifically absent are powers over:

- governance of religion
- training the militia and appointing militia officers
- control over local government
- most crimes
- state justice systems
- family affairs
- real property titles and conveyances
- wills and inheritance
- the promotion of useful arts in ways other than granting patents and copyrights
- control of personal property outside of commerce
- governance of the law of torts and contracts, except in suits between citizens of different states
- education
- services for the poor and unfortunate
- licensing of taverns
- roads other than post roads
- ferries and bridges
- regulation of fisheries, farms, and other business enterprises.

After the Constitutional Convention of 1787, Benjamin Franklin was asked what form of government the delegates had created. He replied "A *Republic*, sir, if you can keep it."

Let's take a closer look at the government our Founders created.

The Constitution is the fundamental law of the Union of the independent and sovereign *States*. Starting with the original 13 colonies, the Union now includes 50 States. The Union, as represented by the Federal Government, also owns an additional six territories or possessions. They are: Puerto Rico, the US Virgin Islands, American Samoa, Guam, the Northern Marianas - and the District of Columbia. Barak Obama, when running for President, incorrectly stated that there were 56 states. There are, in fact, 50 states and 6 territories, or 56 jurisdictions that issue driver's licenses.

As these territories are not *States*, those parts of the Constitution that reserve powers to the States do not apply. So, American citizens who live in these territories cannot vote for President, and the territories do not have Senators or voting Representatives. Moreover, some of their individual rights are not recognized under the Bill of Rights, when it specifically mentions rights granted to citizens of the States.

So, various parts of the US Constitution apply differently to American Citizens depending upon whether they live in a territory or a State. The Constitution also does not protect the rights of a non-citizen outside the United States - such as a foreign terrorist. This, of course, can be changed through a Constitutional Amendment in the future, but to date, no such proposed amendment has ever been successfully voted out of Congress.

Prior to the creation of the United States, nation states were mostly dictatorships or kingdoms. A few, like England, had established independent parliaments through long and bloody battles fought over hundreds of years. The Magna Carta, which granted the first partial freedoms to the English nobility in their battles with the King, forms the basis of the American system of the citizen's individual rights.

Over time, the English government separated itself from the King's power, but the parliamentary system of democracy created only a few checks-and-balances to protect against ruthless politicians. Even today, the government's Ministers (of Defense, Foreign Affairs, Home Affairs, Health and Treasury, for example) are simply Members of Parliament (MPs) selected from the winning political party which controls the most seats in the House of Commons. They are, simultaneously, MPs representing their individual voters, and national government Department heads. And the main party leader takes on the role of the "Prime Minister", controlling both the House of Commons' legislative and the Government's executive branches.

The Chief Justice is also appointed by the Prime Minister. The "Law Lords", or Supreme Court, are made up of members of the upper house of the legislature, the House of Lords, many of whom are now directly appointed by the Prime Minister himself.   So, almost all power is tightly concentrated in the hands of one person. This system worked well during World War II when Prime Minister Winston Churchill was fighting the Nazi's. At other times, the ruler running the government can do a great deal of damage to undermine or destroy the rights of the citizen.

The parliamentary system of democracy clearly did not provide enough separation of power for our American Founders. So, they invented a three-branch presidential system instead.

Under the Constitution, there are two equal houses of legislators, the Senate and the House of Representatives. Laws are jointly created by both bodies before they are sent to the third branch, the Executive, for signature.

Members of the House were (and still are) elected by the individual votes of the citizens of their local district on a representative basis, according to population. Members of the Senate were originally elected by each Senator's home state legislature, two Senators per state[9]. The President was (and still is) elected by the College of Electors, a body in which each state has at least three members.

Originally, the Electors were appointed by each sovereign State government and sent onward to Washington to represent their elected government's interests. They were not easy to corrupt. Over the years, the Electors from a State have been taken over by the political party that garners the most popular votes for President in that State.

When the Constitution was created, political parties did not exist, and consequently, there were no direct checks-and-balances built into in the Constitution to prevent abuses when one political party seized control of Congress and the presidency. Whenever this happens, the freedoms and liberties of the American people tend to suffer because there is no opposing check to balance the ruling party's drive for power.

President George Washington, in his Farewell Address to the People of the United States[10], warned against allowing political parties to capture the power of the Federal Government:

"One of the expedients of party to acquire influence, within particular districts, is to misrepresent the opinions and aims of other districts. You cannot shield yourselves too much against the jealousies and heart burnings which spring from these misrepresentations; they tend to render alien to each other those who ought to be bound together by fraternal affection."

To create a law, both the Senate and the House need to pass their respective bills. Since they are invariably different, and members of each chamber must then work out the differences in a compromise give-and-take joint committee, before the final proposed law can be submitted to the President for his confirming signature. Moreover, the President has the ability to veto any legislation submitted to him. Overriding his veto takes a lot of effort: two-thirds of the members of both legislative bodies must vote in agreement. Only the House can propose spending bills, and all treaties signed by the President must be approved by a two-thirds majority of the Senate. Thus, if the current President signs a "Global Warming Treaty", it would not carry the force of law unless 67 Senators voted to confirm it.

So the system can still function as intended, as long as no one political party has control of both the Congress and the presidency.

Unlike Progressive ideology, the Constitution recognizes that the most power over our lives is reserved to ourselves or to our individual states. To make this absolutely clear, they repeated it explicitly in the 10th Amendment.

The least power was handed over by the people to the Federal Government. Just enough power was transferred away from the individual colonies to the new union of these states, the "United States", to do the things jointly that each couldn't do individually. These included raising a common army and resolving trade and tariff issues between the sovereign states – not IRS agents checking to make sure you complied with ObamaCare's individual mandate to carry insurance coverage.

Key Concepts:

> The Constitution creates a federal government of limited, express powers.

> All the powers not delegated to the federal government are reserved to the people or State governments.

> Both the Constitution and the Bill of Rights protect the citizen from the government, not the other way round.

> The Constitution creates checks and balances over power shared among the three branches of the federal government, and between the federal and state governments.

▷ The Constitution also protects the rights of the sole individual against the power of the raw mob. "We'll give him a fair trial and then we'll hang him" is not allowed. A Republican, not a Democratic, form of government was created.

Quote:

"No man is good enough to govern another man without that other's consent." -Abraham Lincoln

Slogan & Bumper Sticker Ideas:

The Right to Health Care, Welfare, and a Job? Where is That in the Constitution?

Governments don't have rights – People do!

Groups don't have rights – Individuals do!

Chapter 5

Life, Liberty & the Pursuit of Happiness

By the time the Constitution was finally ratified on Wednesday, March 4, 1789, it had become clear that its primary purpose, to protect the inalienable rights of it citizens, might be misinterpreted in the future by people who were not present at its creation. Consequently, the Bill of Rights, was submitted as a package of 10 Amendments to the States, who voted their approval and ratification effective December 15, 1791. Already during that short 2-1/2 year period, rights which had been assumed by the Founders to be inviolate and inalienable were already coming under threat by the young Federal Government. Some historians observe that had the Bill of Rights been proposed a mere 10 years later, many of them would not have passed.

The Bill of Rights represents the genius of Thomas Jefferson and James Madison. They are the real basis of our individual freedoms which so many Americans take for granted. They were created to protect the citizens of the United States against the awesome powers of the United States Federal Government. They were designed to enable people not to fear their government.

Unfortunately, over the years, many have been whittled away by the Federal Government which is charged with enforcing them to protect the people. Some have been outright ignored. Some been reinterpreted by an activist Supreme Court, a role never contemplated by the Founding Fathers. The Bill of Rights may be slowly dying a death of a thousand cuts. But it still exists even if it is often ignored by Progressives in Congress, the Presidency and the Courts. And it can be brought back to life by individuals working together, especially with their State governments.

The 1st Amendment provides for protection of freedom of speech, freedom of the press, freedom to practice any religion, and freedom to peacefully assemble. The government cannot abolish or overrule these freedoms.

The 2nd Amendment says *"the right of the people to keep and bear Arms, shall not be infringed"*. This means that you can own your own gun to defend yourself against external and internal invaders. The Founding Fathers also observed in the Declaration of Independence that if the people have been reduced to live *"under absolute Despotism, it is their Right, it is their Duty, to throw off such Government, and to provide new Guards for their future Security".*

These are scary words for some.

Forty-one States now provide for "must-issue" concealed weapons permits to law-abiding people (the 9 major socialist states including California, New York, Illinois, Massachusetts, etc. forbid their average citizen from carrying weapons to protect themselves). And the National Rifle Association points out that the millions of people who hold concealed weapons permits have the lowest gun injuries and best safety records. It is thought that not a single permit holder has been convicted of a serious crime. However, most Progressive attorneys and politicians fear that the 100 million Americans who own guns are dangerous and may rise up in rebellion against the Federal Government. While these fears are themselves silly and a bit irrational, they do serve the limited but useful role of checking some of the more outrageous grabs for power that Progressive politicians have been making.

The 3rd Amendment prevents the Federal Government from putting its soldiers except in time of War. And war has to be declared by Congress to make it official.

The 4th Amendment prevents the Federal Government from searching and seizing you or your property without probable cause and a Court order.

The 5th Amendment protects you against being forced by the government to testify against yourself. During the middle ages, kings would extract confessions from innocent people by torturing them to talk. Then when they signed a "confession" under torture, the bogus confession was then used to hang them. This nasty trick is still used by many totalitarian dictatorships throughout the world today. But the 5th Amendment does far more. It prevents the government from seizing your property for its own use without "just compensation".

The 6th Amendment provides for your protection when arrested by the government and brought to trial. It calls for an impartial jury trial (they can't all be policemen), and you have a right to know the details of the crime you are accused of, you have a right to examine the witnesses against you, to call your own witnesses, and to have your own defense counsel.

The 7th Amendment gives you the right to demand a jury trial of your peers in any matter where the value in controversy exceeds twenty dollars, and their decision is final. Most modern countries do not recognize such a right for their own citizens. This includes the 27 countries in the European Union and most English-speaking countries. The US is unique in allowing jury trials to protect people's property. Now you know why there are so many attorneys and courts in the United States compared to other countries!

The 8th Amendment prevents cruel or unusual punishment (you can't be whipped) or excessive bail or fines to be imposed against you by the government Court.

The 9th Amendment says that *"the enumeration in the Constitution of certain rights shall not be construed to deny or disparage others retained by the people"*. In other words, just because specific rights of the people are spelled out in the first eight Amendments doesn't mean that the hundreds of other rights that individual citizens have do not exist or can be taken away by the Federal Government. Just because they're not listed above doesn't mean that they don't exist.

Unfortunately, this Amendment is ignored by the Federal Government whenever it is convenient. For example, every individual has an absolute right to personal privacy. Yet the Federal Government through its spy and police agencies passes laws allowing people's cell phones, telephones, e-mails, Internet activities and other electronic communications to be monitored and recorded, without Court authorization or notification. The law which created this violation of American's personal rights is called The PATRIOT Act, whose ostensible purpose is to protect American citizens from external terrorist threats. It was hastily rushed into law on October 26, 2001, barely weeks after the 9/11 tragedy, having handily been waiting to be pulled out of a desk drawer in the White House.

The first 9 Amendments were created to protect the individual citizen from the excess power of the Federal Government. The 10th Amendments was written to protect the sovereign States from the excessive power of the central Federal Government. It was perhaps the first to be ignored by Washington and is today studied more for its historical value than it's weak power.

The 10th Amendment says *"the powers not delegated to the United States by the Constitution, nor prohibited by it to the States, are reserved to the States respectively, or to the people"*. This means that what's not included inside the four corners of the Constitution, written down in the document itself, cannot be done by the Federal Government. So, Federal Agencies not listed in the Constitution, like the Department of Agriculture, EPA, Energy Department, Commerce Department, etc., are not allowed.

Such agencies can be set up by the States themselves, of course, and many States have, in fact, created similar state agencies which mirror their Federal cousins. For example, California has its own Environmental Protection Agency which often passes pollution laws which are tougher than the Federal Government.

During the Progressive four-term presidency of Franklin D. Roosevelt, Jr., FDR rammed through legislation and "broke the back" of the Supreme Court by threatening to double its size and immediately appoint his own cronies as new justices that would vote for anything he asked. The Supreme Court blinked, and re-interpreted the so-called "Commerce Clause" of the Constitution to allow the Federal Government to step in to take over the powers of the States whenever it politically felt like it. The 10th Amendment was mortally wounded.

With the ratification of the 14th Amendment on July 9, 1868, after the Civil War had ended, the Bill of Rights and Federal protections provided to American citizens was extended by the States over themselves. Thus, no State could force someone to testify against themselves if their state laws previously allowed it. Individual rights increased significantly for citizens, in particular the newly-freed slaves who were now included under the protections of the Constitution. Supreme Courts have also occasionally pulled back the Federal Government's all-reaching powers.

But the battle continues.

There is an unending tug-and-pull between the States and the Federal Government. There is another unending pull between the individual and the government at all levels. All governments think that they are too small. All want more money, more employees, and more power so that they can "serve the people". Once a critical mass has been reached, the people get lost in the shuffle and the government winds up serving special interest group after special interest group. And the biggest special interest group in today's United States is the Federal Government itself. The critical mass was reached a long time ago, perhaps going all the way back to 1913 - with the creation of the Federal Income Tax, and the Federal Reserve System of fiat money.

Key Concepts:

> The Bill of Rights limits the government's ability to regulate you, the private citizen.

> All governments think they are too small, and should grow to better

"serve the people."

➢ Once a government or its agencies start growing it is almost impossible to shrink them.

Quotes:

"The enumeration in the Constitution, of certain rights, shall not be construed to deny or disparage others retained by the people." -The Ninth Amendment to the US Constitution

"The powers not delegated to the United States by the Constitution, nor prohibited by it to the States, are reserved to the States respectively, or to the people." -The Tenth Amendment to the US Constitution

Slogan & Bumper Sticker Ideas:

> The Only Things Certain in Life Are Death, Taxes, and Growth in Government!

> Need a Job? Check out the Feds – They Do a Volume Business!

Chapter 6

The Utopian Deception:
Socialism, Marxism/Communism, Fascism, Progressivism

BIG BROTHER IS WATCHING YOU

Over the centuries many "*ism's*" have sprung up to entice people into supporting this Utopia or that Utopia in the belief that a better, more just and freer world can be created. Snake oil salesmen, politicians and philosophers have set up their soap box to sell people on how things should be. Most of these ism's have died out without harming too many people. Often, they faded away when their charismatic leader died.

But there are a few particularly nasty *ism's* which have caught the mind of wanna-be dictators, and are particularly popular to recycle now and then. When they do catch on with the general public, they do enormous damage to morality, freedom and wealth. Like the seasonal flu, they keep mutating over the years, and are difficult to eliminate without a well educated population. Last count, the totalitarian *ism's* of the 20th century killed over 100 million people.

The more virulent *ism's* are: Socialism, Marxism, Communism, Fascism, Progressivism and Corporativism. All are forms of totalitarianism which is the enemy of the individual and individual liberties.

People who wish to push their particular ism over others can't succeed in a free society of open ideas. They need the help of the State to force their will on others. By capturing control of the State, they can use it's police powers to change the form of government into their Utopian ideal.

Government:

Government by definition is an organization of one or more people in control of the administrative apparatus of the *State*. Government is the dominant decision-making and law-passing arm of the State.

Government is often confused with the State. They are not synonyms. A government can be fully voluntary in creation and operation. However, as most governments are usually in control of a "State" and exercise the powers of a State, they are often practically perceived as being interchangeable.

The State:

The State has been defined by the renowned political economist and philosopher Max Weber as the organization that holds a monopoly in the "legal" (or "legitimate") use of violence within its territory to enforce its laws over the people who live within its territory.

The State is the only collection of individuals which is not voluntary. It is, by definition, coercive. All other forms of human collective membership are voluntary. This includes churches, the workplace, sports & other clubs, schools (non-government), friendship societies and charities. Only through the ultimate barrel of a gun can the State enforce its laws on an individual.

Thus the State which intrudes the least on the personal liberties and individual freedoms of its citizens is the one which is the best: it is the one which does the least harm as it goes about its business of enforcing its laws. The Just State is one which takes no side in a conflict between its citizens, administering its laws impartially and fairly. The unjust State is one in which everything has been criminalized, that is, every transgression of a law is a direct attack on the State itself and must be punished by imprisonment or death to the individual.

The State which has the most voluntary cooperation of its citizens is the one which is least feared. This State is usually constructed as a Democracy in which the individual citizens themselves have the ability through their collective vote to elect the members of the Government.

Many of the founding fathers thought of the State as a necessary evil. The bottom line: the smallest State is the State that does the least damage.

Winston Churchill observed: "It has been said that democracy is the worst form of government except all the others that have been tried."

Unlike the *ism's*, the *Free-Enterprise System* is the one arrangement of individuals which springs up naturally wherever it is given a chance.   Even in the saddest days of a totalitarian regime like the present-day North Korea or Cuba, small and free "black markets" have sprung up.   Here the people can come together to buy and sell the minimum necessities of life, like food, which the State cannot provide with it's failed *ism*.   This tiny form of *Capitalism* makes life basely tolerable for those citizens locked inside their totalitarian prison.

Capitalism:

Capitalism is an economic system in which goods and services ("property") are produced, exchanged and owned by individuals with minimal governmental regulation.

Some synonyms for Capitalism are Free Enterprise, Private Enterprise, Free Market, and Entrepreneurship.

Both *Morality* (some call it Ethics) and *Economics* are intimately related.   Both are concerned with human action: our personal conduct, and our personal decisions or choices we make. Capitalism respects individual property rights and thus is the economic system which most closely adheres to the *Two Fundamental Laws* of life.   To be a true capitalist, or entrepreneur requires the highest moral calling.

Capitalism itself may be subdivided into: (1) private property, (2) free markets, (3) competition, (4) division and combination of labor, and (5) social cooperation. They are all mutually dependent. *Private property* means one's own personal property in consumption goods (such as a car, house, pair of shoes). It also means the private ownership of the "means of production", such as farms and factories, movie studios and book publishers.

Capitalism is unique in that it takes advantage of each person's self-interest, and harnesses them to production and exchange which benefit other people. The famous Capitalist motto is: *"find a need and fill it"*. To the Capitalist, the world is a wonderful place of discerning consumers who want to buy producer's goods in a competitive market Capitalism is the natural system of the marketplace which springs up wherever farmers, merchants, and traders set up their market stalls. It is a give-and-take system of individual buyers and sellers.

In a free market, both the seller and the buyer come away feeling good about the transaction. The buyer got something he wanted more than his money, and the seller gets money to be able to buy other things he wanted more than his product. Economists call this a "win-win scenario" where both sides benefit.

Adam Smith understood the benefits of Capitalism in 1776, when he wrote in his famous Wealth of Nations:

> "The annual revenue of every society is always precisely equal to the exchangeable value of the whole annual produce of the industry, or rather is precisely the same thing with that exchangeable value. As every individual, therefore, endeavors as much as he can both to employ his capital in the support of domestic industry, and so to direct that industry that its produce may be of the greatest value; every individual necessarily labors to render the annual revenue of the society as great as he can. He generally, indeed, neither intends to promote the public interest, nor knows how much he is promoting it. By preferring the support of domestic to that of foreign industry, he intends only his own security; and by directing that industry in such a manner as its produce may be of the greatest value, he intends only his own gain, and he is in this, as in many other cases, led by an invisible hand to promote an end which was no part of his intention. Nor is it always the worse for the society that it was no part of it. By pursuing his own interest he frequently promotes that of the society more efficiently than when he really intends to promote it."

In the Capitalist, or free-market system, the free individual is the centerpiece of society. Society forms voluntary groups to accomplish common goals for the specific interest of each member of the group. Coercion, either by armed thugs or the government is not allowed. A minimum government is established to accomplish only those things that it is recognized cannot be done by any voluntary group. These include national defense and, usually, the establishment of an independent court system operating under a tight "rule of law" to ensure that no one individual or group, including the government, can gain control of the free marketplace to the disadvantage of any other.

Capitalism is the system of competition. It is the system which gives the consumer the most choices, the best quality, the least expensive products. Why? Because competition weeds out the crooks and sellers of shoddy goods as fast as word gets around. And it works. *"My Word is My Bond"* has been the motto of the London Stock Exchange for over 200 years. It could as easily be the motto for the Capitalist system. In a Capitalist economy, there is a high degree of trust between buyer and seller. Reputations mean something, and Brand Names are valued.

The Capitalist system wasn't designed by some philosopher. It naturally sprung to life to fill a need of real people, just as the English language itself wasn't invented by the aristocrat elites. They spoke structured Latin, or French at high table. They were the Lords and Ladies. They owned the serfs and slaves. The street merchants and common folk spoke give-and-take make-up-a-word-when-needed English. It seems that English and Capitalism go hand-in-hand. Perhaps that's why English has become the language of business and commerce throughout the world. And English is the language of ideas and intellectual property. Over 70% of the books, movies, magazines, TV shows, & Internet data bases are in English.

When the free market is manipulated by government-sponsored monopolies, hindered by over-regulation, and distorted by state laws, it is always the consumer who suffers most. When the government becomes corrupted, it is usually a tiny band of crooked producers who buy the politicians votes. When the government completely gets into bed with industry, competition is made illegal, and the quality of life deteriorates. With enough government interference, the Capitalist free market system of competition and free trade can be destroyed altogether. By then, the country has usually collapsed by foolishly following an 'ism'.

Totalitarianism:

Totalitarianism (or *totalitarian rule*) is a political system that, according to Wikipedia, *"strives to regulate nearly every aspect of public and private life.* Totalitarian regimes or movements maintain themselves in political power by means of an official all-embracing ideology and propaganda disseminated through the state-controlled mass media, a single party (usually) that controls the state, personality cults, control over the economy, regulation and restriction of free discussion and criticism, the use of mass surveillance", etc.

Benito Mussolini, the Italian dictator during WWII, popularized the concept of totalitarianism, and early 20th-century American Progressives like Presidents Woodrow Wilson and Franklin D. Roosevelt, Jr. were infatuated by it. Totalitarian dictators are often attracted to Socialism and Fascism because in both economic systems the dictator is ensured that he will always remain on top by suppressing the economic freedom and confiscating the wealth of his subjects.

Socialism:

Socialism is a system of social organization by which the means of production and distribution ("property") are owned, managed, and controlled by the government, through the use of force. Socialism is not voluntary. But it does have a great-sounding ring to its name. It just sounds so downright friendly and helping. The iron fist hidden inside the velvet glove is usually not noticed until later.

Synonyms: Collectivism, Communism, Communalism, Marxism, Leninism, Maoism.

French philosophers of the 18th Century launched an argument against private property using John Locke's theory of knowledge. John Locke was the father of classical liberalism. They argued that everything that we are is simply a result of our experiences, not some fundamental set of universal truths. Thus, through new laws and state-run education human beings can be changed.

They theorized that property is the root of all evil, and therefore through its abolition people can be totally "socialized". People will then no longer desire to own anything, but will want to share everything. This became the basis of modern "socialism" as taught by Marx. For Marx, the definition of socialism or "communism" as he preferred to call it, was simply the abolition of all private property and its forced transfer to the State, a direct violation of both of the two fundamental Laws of Life.

It's not surprising that failed French philosophers thought up modern Socialism. They also created the conditions for "The Terrors". They were the people who were responsible for the French Revolution, the revolt which launched the mass use of the Guillotine, ultimately killing off themselves in the process. The end result was the emergence of the world's greatest dictator at that time: Napoleon. It took war with England to undo the damage. In the process, France lost a bit of her soul and has never completely thrown off the yoke of Socialism.

"Force cannot change Right", Thomas Jefferson.

Marxism/Communism/Maoism:

If Socialism is a form of "Marxism Lite", then Marxism is a form of "Socialism Heavy" - and very heavy indeed. Marxism is the logical and ultimate extension of Social-ism to its state-glorifying conclusion. Under Marxism, all the means of production are owned by the State. TV, Radio, the Press are official State Organs. No dissenting opinion is allowed. The "Labor Union" is a State Agency, along

with the Red Cross and the Church (if allowed). The State is usually officially atheist, as Marx himself called religion "the Opiate of the People", and should be banned.

Musicians, actors, writers must get permission from the State to publish their works. Inventors must invent products "for the good of the people". Private innovation not following the State's Dictator-in-Chief is frowned upon or punished. The Ruler appoints himself for life, and gives himself a grandiose name like "Most Beloved" or "Dear Leader". Since there is only one Party, the Party is above the government. The Party controls all. Its Secret Police track everyone. People are paid to inform against their neighbors, and children against their parents. Prison Camps and "re-education camps" are established to punish anyone who disagrees. Firing squads and psychiatric hospitals tame the remaining few freedom lovers.

Welcome to hell. When you think of Marxism, think of Pol Pot's Cambodia or Stalin's USSR, or Mao's China, or Kim Jong-il's North Korea. Collectively, they murdered over 100 million people.

Life under a Marxist state is brutal, squalid, and usually short for its citizens. Living without hope, in Communist Russia men drank themselves into early graves. As recently as 1990, the average citizen died in his mid-50's, and that age was falling. The Communist Party never allows more than 5% of the population to join it. Who would be left to rule over if everyone were a member of the party elite? In the USSR, at the peak of the Communists' rule, the Party never had more than 3-1/2 % of the population in its cadres. Of course, the Grand Ruler and his elite syncopates live rich lives separated from the people who have been reduced to slaves or serfs.

Because competition and free trade are not allowed, and no one can own any property except the State, there is no incentive to produce new goods or services or even to work, as everyone is guaranteed a "job for life". Also, everyone must work at that job, and live in the government-owned flat assigned, and in the city assigned to them to live. Travel requires internal passports and permission to go from city to city. No one is allowed to leave the country except loyal members of the elite ruling class.

Under Communism as a system of economics, there is no need for the word "profit" to exist, as everything is owned by the State, or as the Dictator says, "the People". In fact, in the USSR, the word "profit" was even excised from the Russian language dictionary.

In this make-believe Kafkaesque dysfunctional economy, where production is enforced through fear and terror, four rules or *truths* immediately surface. Understand them, and you completely understand how Communism works.

The four economic truths of all Communist societies:

1) There is no relationship between what something costs and what it sells for (so shoddy goods abound)

2) There is no relationship between supply and demand (shortages are everywhere)

3) There is no relationship between time and money (stand in line, shut up, and wait)

4) Paper is more important than people ("may I see your papers Comrade?")

Apply these rules to an entire economy and you will create a system which ultimately destroys itself. Unfortunately, as Marxist regimes are notoriously violent against their own people, they are also paranoid of invasion from outside. So Communist countries are dangerous to the peaceful existence of their neighbors.

Fortunately, with a lot of bribery, regular people can just get by. For Communist Party members, life is much better. They have their own special party hospitals, special party stores, special party vacation parks, special party farms - even special party telephones.

Given the fact that Communism has been "voluntarily" tried in dozens of countries over the past 100 years, and has failed in every one of them, it's puzzling that some students in colleges and universities want to bring Marxism, or it's baby brother, Socialism, to the United States. Are they just plain evil too? No, just ignorant. They're too young to know the horrors of the USSR or Mao's China or Pol Pot's Cambodia. They've never visited North Korea. They can't get in.

Fascism:

Wikipedia defines Fascism as "a radical and authoritarian nationalist political ideology and a Corporatist economic ideology" While many people think of Fascism as a "right-wing" movement, it is, in fact a left-wing phenomena, a form of "Totalitarianism" akin to Socialism, or Marxism.

The word "fascism" comes from the Latin root "fasces", symbolizing the State's power from the Roman Empire onwards. The Progressive President, Woodrow Wilson even had the fascist symbol placed on the reverse of the Winged Liberty Head (Mercury) Dime which was used during WWI in 1916 through the end of WWII in 1945. It was replaced with the present Dime showing the image of Progressive President Franklin Roosevelt on its obverse (front) side.

The full name of the German NAZI party was the "National *Socialist* German Workers Party". It was wildly admired by people on both sides of the Atlantic as a means of recovering from the "Great Depression", which began in 1929. Many prominent American figures were proponents of fascism being adopted in the United States, until just before the US was attacked by the Japanese at Pearl Harbor. They included leading members of Congress - and even President Franklin D. Roosevelt, Jr.

After the US joined the war against the NAZI's they stopped talking about the glories of Fascism. They simply modified the Fascist approach to control by minimizing the thugs and jackboots, although the US did build prison camps and rounded up American citizens of Japanese, Italian and German descent and locked them up behind barbed wire.

To the little guy, Fascism and Communism look the same. The same secret police, the same prison camps, the same Dictator, the same boot is stepping on the back of his neck.

Of course, under Communism, everything is owned by the State - and controlled by a Party elite. The wealth of the State goes to benefit the elite. What little is left over is then spread around on the citizen-serfs.

Under Fascism, everything is owned by giant State-owned and "independent" conglomerates - controlled by a Party elite. The wealth of the Corporations goes to benefit the elite. What little is left over is then spread around on the citizen-serfs.

See the difference? Thought not.

Corporatism:

In an attempt to minimize the visible brutal use of force, advanced Socialist and Fascist strategists have developed a new alternative. Former Communist countries like the USSR and Red China are moving toward Corporatism as a slicker way of keeping their own elites in power. Even the ordinary citizen is allowed to make money, and a form of tightly-regulated Mixed Economy (part Capitalist, Part Totalitarian) is created. Often, controls over the people take the form of "protections for your own good" A Nanny-State and Big Brother Surveillance State is created.

Corporatism is defined by Wikipedia as: "a system of economic, political, and social organization where social groups or interest groups, such as business, ethnic, farmer, labor, military, or patronage groups, are joined together under a common governing jurisdiction to try to achieve societal harmony and promote coordinated development".

Corporatism is a practice, "whereby a state, through the process of licensing and regulating officially-incorporated social, religious, economic, or popular organizations, effectively co-opts their leadership or circumscribes their ability to challenge state authority by establishing the state as the source of their legitimacy, as well as sometimes running them, either directly or indirectly through corporations."

"Liberal Fascism" is often thought of as a form of friendly Corporatism. That is, it is "fascism light" with tight top-down control over all aspects of the society, government ownership, in conjunction with big-business of the banking, insurance, financial, heavy-industry, and media sectors, without the "boot jack" suppression of the popular descent that the NAZI form of Fascism was famous for.

Progressivism:

In the United States, the word "Progressive" means something different than it does in Europe. In the US, the Progressive Party was formed by President Teddy Roosevelt after he lost his re-election campaign for the Republican Party. Then Democrat President Woodrow Wilson extended the *"Progressive"* ideas of big government and big business even further.

Over the years, the Progressives have slowly built up their power and influence inside both major political parties. They advocate Corporatism and Socialism, where the government takes over failing businesses in the free market to "save jobs". They then install their own elite "Czars" to run these government-owned businesses. Of course, the reason the businesses failed in the first place was because of the policies and laws Progressives previously passed in Congress.

These laws systematically distorted the free market by manipulating the money supply, preventing competition in the workplace, and creating monopoly protection for bloated and antiquated industry.

Progressivism is simply totalitarianism in slow motion. The strategy of "nudging" was developed by Richard Cloward and Frances Fox Piven, then both sociologists and political activists at Columbia University. Progressivism separated itself from the violent path of revolutionary Marxism, replacing it by a "gentler" form where the iron fist is kept concealed inside a velvet glove.

Progressivism quickly deteriorates into cronyism and corrupt government. Laws are applied selectively against their enemies and ignored when their friends violate them. Friends of a Progressive government can make a fortune with special sweet-heart deals, especially in the banking and finance industries. Progressives have a love affair with big business. They are suspicious of small business and the single entrepreneur.

Progressive Administrations are noted for hiring the least number of people who actually worked for a living in business. Progressives especially avoid people who have actually built and run their own businesses and have real-world hands-on experience.

Modern "progressives" support a form of "liberal fascism", or fascism with a happy face, as described by Jonah Goldberg in his best-selling book, *Liberal Fascism*. Perhaps this brand of friendly politically-correct fascism is most like Peronism, formulated by the Argentina President Juan Peron as a populist movement.

As their failures in mismanaging the economy and government become clearer, Progressives then attempt to move to Corporatism or Fascism. Debate is squashed as the Media is told to shut up or report the "party line". Alternative media is closed down or regulated out of business.

Progressivism has one thing in common with all the other "*isms*". Progressives are people who seek power over other people's lives. They think they are smarter than the ordinary citizen-serf. And once in power, they want to change the rules to stay in power.

Like any totalitarian, they pass laws to suppress free speech. They set up big-brother controls and nanny-state "nudges". Don't do this, don't do that. Eat this, don't smoke that, think this way, don't vote that way. And they ruthlessly attack and ridicule anyone who disagrees with them. In a Progressive State, there's only one right way, theirs.

Progressives don't believe in the individual, or democracy. They are narcissistic power-mad control freaks. If polls show that 80% of the people disagree with them, then the people are wrong and will just have to be "re-educated" to think the correct way. That's why Progressives are in favor of government-run schools and vehemently against home schooling.

Ultimately, the hubris which the Progressive is cursed with is the desire to replace God with himself. That's why to the Progressive, ethics and morality are situational. Since all cultures are equal in a multicultural society, there is no moral right to condemn a cannibal for cooking and eating another person. Who are we to judge? Western civilization is not superior to primitive neolithic societies.

That's why you don't hear the Progressives screaming about the injustice of female genital mutilation in Africa or women being imprisoned in Burkas or being treated as male chattel in some Muslim countries. The same Progressives ignore the surpression of the Bible and the prohibition of Christian churches and worship in Saudia Arabia, and the stoning to death of a woman found guilty of adultery or being gay (sodomy). Everything is OK everywhere. Hate and violence and mass-murder elsewhere on the planet can co-exist with free love, free sex and same-sex marriages in the US. They can condone "art" in which feces are spread on a painting of the Virgin Mary, but would never think of doing the same thing to Mohammad. Progressives respect all cultures - except their own.

The Mixed Economy:

Unfortunately, no country in the world today is completely Capitalist and therefore completely free. The United States itself is a highly-mixed economy, with much of the "means of production" owned by the State.

Forms of government range from totally individual-oriented free-market (capitalist) to totally government-oriented totalitarian (communist, socialist or fascist). The libertarian test for freedom is simple: Is the government part of the problem or part of the solution? Does its existence increase my personal liberty and freedoms or decrease them?

Using this criteria, the United States today is a mixed-economy. It is part free-market (capitalist) and part socialist (communist). It is easy to demonstrate this. Simply consider what the "government" owns today. First, let's start with The US Postal Service (the Post Office). The USPS employs 25% of all civilian federal workers. But why does it continue to exist and lose money every day? Most people use the alternatives of e-mail via the Internet and faster and often cheaper physical delivery services such as FedEx, UPS, DHL, and others.

At the Federal, State, and Local levels, the amount of property, businesses and assets the governments own is staggering. Most of these services and assets are owned by private industry in places throughout the United States and in other countries. For example, the German post office is now a shareholder-owned company which trades on stock exchanges throughout the world. Its now called Deutche Post DHL, AG.   British Airports Authority, or BAA for short, is now a subsidiary of a Spanish investor-owned company traded worldwide. BAA owns the worlds busiest airport, London's Heathrow, among many others. So why does the Port Authority of New York own Kennedy International?

Here's a quick look of just a few of the government assets owned in the United States:

- The national passenger train company AMTRAK.
- Millions of office & apartment buildings nationwide
- 60% of all the land west of the Rocky Mountains, including
- National Forests, National Parks, National Wildlife lands
- Electric Companies & Nuclear Power Generating Plants (e.g. TVA)
- Water Companies (e.g. San Francisco's Hetch Hetchy System)
- Sewage Systems
- Waste Removal Businesses
- Fire Companies
- Police Departments
- Gas Companies
- Ports & Airports
- Air Traffic Control Centers
- Regional Train Companies throughout the country
- Telephone Companies
- Cable TV Companies
- Bus Lines
- Boats & Ferry Lines
- Bridges, Tunnels & Roads (both free and toll)
- Space Vehicle Launching Systems & Communications
- GPS, Resources, Research & Weather Satellites
- Armament Manufacturers (e.g. armories)
- Nuclear Fuel Manufacturing Plants & Nuclear Reactors
- Research Labs in dozens of technical fields including energy
- Hospitals & Hospital Chains (e.g. Veterans Administration) & Research Labs
- Museums, Parks, Zoos, Libraries, Ball Parks

- Opera Houses, Symphony Halls, Commercial Exhibition & Performance Halls
- Commercial Forest Logging Operations
- Gas, Oil, Thermal and Water Leasing Operations
- Dams, Waterways, Rivers, Canals and Lakes
- Schools: primary, secondary, high school, college & university
- Radio & TV Stations (e.g. Voice of America) broadcasting government programs worldwide
- Printing & Publishing (e.g. General Printing Office GPO), Newspapers, Magazines
- Enforcement Officers (Armed), including: Army, Air Force, Navy, Marines, TSA, FBI, DHS, ATF and local

Other countries, particularly in the European Union, have been selling off their state-owned assets for decades in a clear reversal of this trend.

Recently, however, the United States has moved further toward the process of extending government control either indirectly or directly over a far greater segment of the private sector. Nationalization, either through controlling loans or stock ownership (preferred or common shares) has enabled the Federal Government to own and control:

Major federally-chartered banks like CitiBank

Major insurance companies like AIG

General Motors and other automobile-industry companies

Proposed government nationalization of other sectors include the health care industry and the energy industry, as well as Federal Government expansion of national control over the States through the use of loan guarantees.

Progressive badly mis-managed States such as California are bankrupt. California itself owes over $100 billion in dodgy loans. As the Progressive agenda continues in Washington, the Federal Government will continue to "guarantee" bankrupt state debts, using the ability of the US Treasury to issue more Treasury Bills (IOU's) which the Federal Reserve then buys up with printing-press fiat money.

By using the power of government domain coupled with the power of sovereign (monopoly) issued money, the process of moving from a freer independent economy to a more controlled "corporatist" economy can be accelerated. This strategy was proposed at the turn of the 20th century by both Presidents Teddy Roosevelt and Woodrow Wilson, a Republican and Democrat, respectively.

The systematic reduction of the free market economy and the increase of state-owned businesses results, of course, in a collapse of GDP, decrease in individual liberties - especially among those people opposed to the government's controls and policies, and civil strife. Countries that have followed this sad route often end up as military dictatorships. South America has seen dozens over the years. Venezuela is going this route today. This is one of the universally consistent outcomes of ultimate conversion of a mixed-economy to a state-dominated or controlled economy.

Key Concepts:

> Government is a collection of people in control of the apparatus of the State.

> The State is the only group of people that is "legally" ("legitimately") allowed to use violence to enforce its laws.

> Totalitarianism destroys an individual's initiative and freedom, and can be achieved through any system that empowers the State at the expense of the private sector.

Quote:

"A government big enough to supply you with everything you need, is a government big enough to take away everything that you have." -Thomas Jefferson

Slogan & Bumper Sticker Ideas:

First the Banks. Then the Car Companies. Now Health Care! What's Next?!

A Chicken in Every Pot, and a Camera in Every Bedroom!

Chapter 7

Ensuring Personal Liberty & Freedom:
Free Markets & Free Minds

An economic system is the result of its legal system. Economic systems vary between those in which the individual is king to those in which the state is king. In other words, they can be constructed as systems in which economic power flows from the grass roots upward or downward from the ruler on top.

The best economic model is "Austrian Economics", which represents the most free market economic understanding of human interaction. It also appears to be most in tune with the understandings of the Declaration of Independence and our constitutional structure of "checks and balances". It is a model which encourages competition and discourages corruption.

Its founders were from Austria, including Ludwig Von Mises and F.A. Hayek, who received the Nobel Prize in 1974. The "Chicago School" of Economics as represented by Milton Friedman (1976 Nobel Prize in Economics) and numerous Austrian School "think tanks" such as the Heritage Foundation *www.Heritage.org*, the CATO Institute *www.Cato.org*, and the Hoover Institution *www.Hoover.org* continue on this tradition.

Every year the Heritage Foundation, in conjunction with the Wall Street Journal, publishes its Index of Economic Freedom based primarily on the application of this universal truth country-to-country. An excellent Austrian School source for further information is The Foundation for Economic Education *www.Fee.org*.

FEE maintains an extensive web site and publishes books and articles both on-line and in printed form. Frederic Bastiat's short book, *The Law*, is a must-read for those who want to understand clearly what makes the Law just and a society, in turn, moral.

Economics in One Lesson, by Henry Hazlitt, is a classic fun-to-read book which explains how everything really works. It belongs in everyone's library.

Leonard Read's I, Pencil, is a short essay on how the lowly pencil comes into existence because of the coordinated entrepreneurial efforts of thousands of people in dozens of industries throughout the world.

What Has Government Done to Our Money? by Murray Rothbard; The Road to Serfdom by Friedrich Hayek; and Economics for Real People by Gene Callahan will round out the collection.

About the above books, Congressman Ron Paul from Texas has said:

"If you simply read and comprehend these relatively short texts, you will know far more than most educated people about economics and government. You certainly will develop a far greater understanding of how supposedly benevolent government policies destroy prosperity. If you care about the future of this country, arm yourself with knowledge and fight back against economic ignorance. We disregard economics and history at our own peril."

You can order printed copies of these books or download most for free as PDF's from the Insider section of our website: *www. RefoundingAmericaBook.com.*

Finally, a really great book - especially for high school kids - is <u>The Adventures of Jonathan Gullible</u>. Now translated into over 50 languages, it is written by Ken Schoolland, Associate Professor of Economics and Political Science at Hawaii Pacific University. Jonathan Gullible sells for $15.95. But you can again download a complete PDF for free at our Insiders section of our website: *www.RefoundingAmericaBook.com*

We'll discuss "Austrian Economics" more in the first four chapters of Part II. For now, it is sufficient to say that in economics, like law, the truest statements are also the clearest.

Henry David Thoreau said that "The law will never make men free; it is men who have got to make the law free." Though self-evident, natural law – the Law of Nature and nature's God – is not self-enforcing. That project requires a sustained effort by dedicated citizens to enact laws that respect man's nature and the world around him. It can be done. In Part III, we'll show you how.

There is one very special event held every July in Las Vegas that you should attend if you can. It's called FreedomFest! It's "the world's largest gathering of free minds", as it's creator Dr. Mark Skousen calls it. Thousands of freedom-loving people come from all over the country to attend.

FreedomFest runs for 3 days of non-stop seminars featuring over 100 speakers who you can talk with up close and personal. Steve Forbes has been known to spend his time mingling with the other attendees for the entire time. It includes an exhibition hall full of libertarian and conservative organizations, lunches and keynote dinners, and coverage by C-SPAN of its many famous authors who talk about their books on economics, personal freedom, and government. And Ron Paul will be there with his *Campaign for Liberty* organization. It's a must-do event, a joyful festival to "pursue life, liberty and happiness". Visit *www.FreedomFest.com* for details. We'll see you there.

Key Concepts:

> Like all forums to exercise freedom, the conditions to allow a free market must be respected in and by law.

> Austrian Economics is the clearest, simplest, and truest explanation of economic behavior.

Quote:

"Underlying most arguments against the free market is a lack of belief in freedom itself." -*Milton Friedman*

Slogan & Bumper Sticker Idea:

I ❤ Austrian Economists

Footnotes to Part I:

[1] *http://en.wikipedia.org/wiki/Property*
[2] *http://en.wikipedia.org/wiki/Soviet_democracy*
[3] *http://www.richardmaybury.com/twolawsA.html*
[4] *http://www.heritage.org/Research/Commentary/2008/01/The-Link-Between-Freedom-Prosperity*
[5] *http://www.richardmaybury.com/chaostanA.html*
[6] *Of course, you can forgo this right to your own life by violating the Second Fundamental Law if you encroach on another person or their property. For example, if you commit the ultimate crime of property theft by killing another person, you have lost your right to control your own body*
[7] *http://en.wikipedia.org/wiki/Kelo_v._City_of_New_London*
[8] *http://en.wikipedia.org/wiki/Quotations_from_Chairman_Mao*
[9] *This important check-and-balance on the Senators was removed when the 17th Amendment changed their election to state-wide "popular" vote, breaking their connection to their own State governments. It has had the effect of turning the Senate into an independent national body representing its own Federal Government interests above those of the sovereign States. It was ratified under Progressive President Woodrow Wilson on April 8, 1913*
[10] *http://avalon.law.yale.edu/18th_century/washing.asp*

PART II: THE CURRENT ISSUES

"Just because you do not take an interest in politics, doesn't mean politics won't take an interest in you."

-Pericles

Think of this section as the "applied principles" part of the book. Through fifteen chapters we discuss the issues that are currently serving as the battleground for freedom vs. oppression. In each chapter, we present the two clearest alternatives to each issue: Progressivism and Classical Liberalism. If you take away only one idea from this part of the book, it should be this: Progressives want Power; Classical Liberals want Freedom. It is that simple. It is that different. And it is always true. We look at fifteen issues, discuss what each side says, and reveal what each really means. For all of these issues the disagreement ultimately comes down to an argument for more power for the government, or more freedom for individuals. It really is that simple.

Chapter 1 explains the death struggle between Marxism and the free market. Though the idea of a free market is fairly new, the truths of its insights are apparent in ancient writings from every culture. Man cannot be made moral by coercion, nor can he flourish if he fears theft from his neighbors. Thus, the best system is one that treats people as rational human beings, applying the law equally to all.

Chapter 2 pulls back the curtain on the Federal Reserve System and its monopoly of fiat money. Since its creation in 1913, the Fed has exercised increasing control over America's money supply, as well as the interest rate. At its whim, the Fed can manipulate the value of the dollar to satisfy whatever private or government interests it deems appropriate. This is not the first time a government-backed banking system held the nation's economy hostage. Like the others, it should be eliminated and resisted from resurrecting.

Chapter 3 describes the road to fiscal ruin we are on thanks to runaway deficit spending by pass-the-buck politicians. If you are familiar with the Bernie Madoff scandal, you understand how a Ponzi scheme works: pay off past creditors with money from new investors. Sound familiar? The same is true with Social Security. Workers today pay for the benefits of today's retirees. The system works as long as you have either an equal number of payers and takers, or more payers than takers. When you don't, the scheme fails. Bernie Madoff is in prison because his Ponzi scheme failed. What happens when Social Security goes bust?

Chapter 4 reveals the lie behind raising taxes. Over the long run, more taxes lead to less production, higher unemployment, and a stagnant economy. People don't like to have their money taken from them. Eventually, they modify their behavior to avoid the pain and frustration of legalized theft. Businesses hire less people, or get out of certain industries with oppressive costs. Fewer people can find jobs, and the jobs that are available pay less, because the amount of compensation is tied to the amount of taxes paid. Finally, economies grind to a halt as companies and jobs migrate overseas to more business (i.e. tax) friendly locales.

Chapter 5 shows you the lengths Progressives are willing to go to secure power. The stories you've heard about voting and census fraud are true. Dead people vote, answer census questionnaires, and in some cases, claim multiple residences. In the 2008 presidential election, the abuse by ACORN was so rampant that several states' attorneys general opened formal investigations. Any abuse in the electoral or census process is inexcusable, but when it changes the outcome of an election or congressional apportionment, the first step towards tyranny has been taken.

Chapter 6 takes a look at political corruption in the government and marketplace. You may be surprised to learn that Progressives *love* Big Business. In fact, many of the top donors to Progressive causes are corporate titans looking to invest in two government options: subsidies and regulation of competitors. Both of these market-distorting outcomes protect the establishment while dooming entrepreneurs. Eventually, our free enterprise system will turn into the crony capitalism of many European countries.

Chapter 7 examines the dirty little secret behind the demise of the mainstream media. They refuse to give consumers the news they want. The popularity of talk radio, Fox News, and online opinion outlets is a direct result of the old line network television and newspaper companies refusing to acknowledge their Progressive bias. When given an alternative, readers and viewers are voting for news content generators that provide information from a perspective they trust.

Chapter 8 stays in the news realm, but pivots towards a constitutional guarantee enjoyed by all members of the media: Freedom of the Press. Like other aspects of life, a free market unfettered with government intrusion should be available for information as well as goods. While there is a limited place regulating certain types of speech, political speech should be free, open, and unafraid of rebuttal. Yet Progressives prefer censorship and control, and silence dissent in countries where they rule.

Chapter 9 peeks behind the words of the Constitution and finds a generation of statesmen intimately concerned with protecting personal privacy from the government's prying eyes. The Colonists experienced a long history of royal abuse in searches, seizures, and arbitrary imprisonment. To guard against these, they drafted not only the Constitution, but also the Bill of Rights. Many of the most famous amendments are directly aimed at checking the government's "right" to know things about its citizens.

Chapter 10 takes a stroll through the education debate. On one side stand Progressives, teachers unions, bureaucrats, and the politicians who fund their dismal performance. On the other side are those who think each student is an individual deserving of as many choices in primary and secondary education as are available at the college level. Parents should have choices how to spend their education dollars to best benefit the most important student: theirs.

Chapter 11 confronts the controversial topic of immigration. Like so many other issues, Progressive policies are distorting the conversation into a debate about quotas for ethnic minorities. No true American wants to turn away an immigrant wanting to pursue a better life in the land of opportunity. The history of American expansion was fueled by immigration, and many of our greatest achievements were won by immigrants. Progressives know that most Americans are inherently open to immigration so long as it leads to integration. But since integration presupposes a shared national identity that is antithetical to the Progressive multi-cultural worldview, Progressives push policies that overwhelm any community's ability to integrate newcomers. These include refusing to police the border, mandating multi-lingual government documents and programs, and expanding the ways people can gain entry through relatives.

Chapter 12 filters through the haze of global warming, and pops the top off cap-and-trade policy. While the recent revelations of intimidation, stonewalling, fraud, and abuse of process coming from the University of East Anglia's Climate Research Unit and the United Nations' Intergovernmental Panel on Climate Change are appalling, they are not surprising. "Climate change" is little more than the most recent attempt by Progressives to redistribute wealth on a global scale. The science is unimportant. Now we know it is also wrong.

Chapter 13 powers through the "energy wars" being waged in the halls of government, and highlights the high stakes lobbying taking place over how we consume energy. For nearly forty years presidents have tried to spur creation of a "green" economy. The problem is, the "green" economy costs too much, so consumers continue to opt for products using natural gas, oil, and coal. Though these resources are cleaner now than before, and abundant throughout the United States, they don't meet the litmus test of "greenness" for Progressives. Instead, Progressives want to heavily subsidize technologies like ethanol, wind, and solar that cannot compete in a free market. They also want to restrict the manufacture of natural gas, oil, and coal to force consumers to pay more money for less available energy.

Chapter 14 scratches under the surface of the healthcare debate, and exposes the lies of socialized medicine. Progressives are fond of denying the failure of their policies elsewhere, claiming that only the implementation was flawed. They'll get it right next time. Except they won't, because they can't. Britain's quality of life has been steadily eroding since its government forced the National Health Service onto the public. Now, wait times, exploding budgets, and treatment rationing are rampant. The same awaits us under Obamacare.

Chapter 15 sets its sights on the Second Amendment; the one that protects all the others. You don't need to be an expert in grammar to understand that the plain language of the amendment guarantees each individual citizen a right to own gun. To think otherwise would have been madness to the founders. They knew that when government has all the guns, no one has any peace. Totalitarian regimes the world over use gun licensing and registration schemes to identify guns before taking them. You have a constitutional right to defend yourself from all enemies; both foreign, and domestic.

Chapter 1

Economics in One Lesson: Marx vs. Adam Smith & Ludwig Von Mises; Freedom vs. Slavery

By definition, "economics" is the study of shortages, and how to balance the demand between goods and services in a real world where demand for a good may be nearly infinite but its supply severely limited. There are only two ways to solve this problem. Either dictate from the top down by the use of rationing and regimentation who shall get what goods, how many, and at what price. Or create a marketplace which allows each individual buyer and seller to independently arrive at the price by freely competing with others. The latter approach mirrors the world of nature, where competition between God's individual creatures and among species is the way the world has been created.

PROGRESSIVES

Much can be learned about an idea from the words its supporters use to communicate it. In economics, there are two basic schools of thought on how to describe society: collectivism and individualism. The collectivists see society as combinations of irreducible groups vying for power. They must be forced into control and submission by the ruling elite. The individualists see society as made up of individual persons, each voluntarily seeking their own self-interest in a friendly marketplace of buyers and sellers.

By nature, Progressives are collectivists. And the most (in)famous types of collectivists are Marxists. If you've ever read the works of Karl Marx or any of his adherents, you'll notice a constant reference to "the masses." In Marxist ideology, the term "masses" refers to the vast swath of people being oppressed by the ruling elite. In theory, the masses are in need of a revolution to throw off the chains of economic slavery so that they can create a worker's paradise where all are treated exactly the same. In practice, the masses trade one set of elites for another.

This is the model used by Progressives. Adopting the language of collectivism, Progressives see the populace as identity groups. Think of the modern Democratic Party. The coalitions that supply its membership are all driven by identity groups claiming to represent the interests of racial minorities, women, homosexuals, unions, environmentalists, and activist business people. Each of these groups is organized for the purpose of securing government preferences like affirmative action, minority business contracts, and regulations favoring their members.

The biggest impact of the collectivist mindset can be seen in the economic arena. In order to enforce his vision of guaranteed equality, Marx popularized the maxim, "from each according to his ability, to each according to his need." This principle breaks the connection between production and compensation. In countries where it is applied, it also breaks the connection between effort and reward. A famous joke in the old Soviet Union was: "they pretend to pay us and we pretend to work". The irony is that even this joke is distorted. In the real world, you contribute your time first, and then you receive your compensation in money for your time already spent.

Ultimately, this rupture between reward and effort modifies behavior for both individuals and groups. Individuals produce less, yet expect more; especially when they see groups successfully lobbying for a greater portion of benefits. For their part, groups become the dominant social force, gobbling up resources because of their "needs," and criticizing opponents as being immoral. In time, the majority of people – whether in groups or as individuals – become takers rather than producers, with the final result being a fight over the table scraps of a once robust economy.

In the collectivist-run economy, this error in understanding how economics works creates terrible distortions and suppresses the normal competition among buyers and sellers.

Since no one can be paid any more money to produce more (for that would be unfair), positive incentives to produce more goods don't exist. Instead, punitive incentives must be employed: work gangs, gulags and exile or death for the shirker. A secret police force must be created to enforce the fear. A bureaucracy or soviet "nomenclature" of deputy-Czars is created to set the prices. Marketplace rules do not apply. Instead, four universal truths become apparent in a Marxist economy:

1) There is no relation between supply and demand.

Supply is set by "5 year plans". Ration cards & queues resolve shortages. Discontent is suppressed by the secret police.

2) There is no relationship between what something costs and what it sells for.

The deputy-Czars set the prices. Charging a higher, or lower, price is a crime.

3) There is no relationship between time and money.

Equal work for equal pay means everyone's time has the same equal value, the lowest common denominator. Since people are paid whether they do good work or poor work, shoddy goods and services abound. Take it or leave it.

4) Paperwork is more important than people.

"My word is my bond" is meaningless. No one is to be trusted as everyone will steal if given a chance, as there are shortages for everything except, perhaps, bullets. Passbooks, ration coupons, residence permits, internal passports exist.

The idea of "making a profit" which can be saved and re-invested in the future is missing from Marxism. Indeed, collectivist regimes like the old USSR are known for their chronic under-investment in capital infrastructure for future growth. Capitalism in its very name recognizes the essential requirement to save up capital to be able to invest in a growing economy.

CLASSICAL LIBERALS

Classical liberals are individualists by nature. They want freedom instead of power, and the only control they desire is over their own decisions. Adam Smith's chief insight was realizing that an individual's self-interest could be turned into a force for achieving the common good if the economic system he participated in was made free. By allowing rational individuals to seek their own enrichment through free trade and capital creation, Smith argued that others would benefit as a result of everyone seeking maximum value.

At its core, free market capitalism is the most dynamic societal engine for bringing people together. Capitalism does not work in a vacuum – you need others to buy, sell, and grow rich. Moreover, capitalism does not reward fraud or shoddy work. A person's reputation for such activity gets around quickly making future trade impossible. Therefore, it is in the capitalist's best interest to observe the First Fundamental Law: do all that you agree to do. A man's word is his bond. Break it, and you've broken your ability to enrich yourself.

Another benefit of capitalism is its basic operating principle: freedom. Capitalism depends on a series of contracts freely entered into for goods and services freely paid for and sold. Coercion, fraud, and even mistakes the unmistaken party should know of are all defenses to forming a contract. Simply, put capitalism cannot work on a slavery model because serfs do not work as hard or as well as free men.

Contrast this with the Progressives' collectivist vision. In the ideal collectivist economy, there is no connection between production and compensation. Marx assumed that in a perfect communist society, there would be enough goods for everyone to be satisfied. But there never are because an individual's needs and desires change. As the Soviet Union proved year after year, accurately anticipating the right amount of goods in advance leads to shortages and overages; never the right amount.

The centralized command-and-control nature of collectivist planning ultimately leads to a culture of dependency on the ruling elite for everything. The system creates a new form of slavery. Instead of being empowered to create wealth and choose how to spend it, individuals are made to plead with the State for the necessities of life, all on the State's terms. The only choices are those the State allows. The only freedoms are those it permits. The result is a nation enslaved into serfdom.

Classical liberals understand that humans cannot be made moral by coercion, nor can they flourish if they fear theft from their neighbors. Acknowledging this, Classical Liberals believe that the best economic system is one that treats people as rational human beings, allowed to seek the betterment of themselves while in the process, bettering others.

The fatal flaw of Marxism denies each person's basic desire to save, invest and own property; accumulating wealth to pass on to his children. The Marxist believes that the economic pie is fixed and finite. Therefore, if one person takes a piece of the pie to eat, he must have taken it away from someone else. In contrast, the Capitalist knows that the pie is ever-expanding. Wealth is created spontaneously and called into existence by individual creativity to "find a need and fill it" coupled with the desires of the buyers in the marketplace to consume. Marxists reject the consumer society and its bounty of plenty. Capitalists encourage choice, competition of ideas, and a free market richly supplied with goods and services.

The question is: which system succeeds best in maximizing the prosperity and wealth of the largest number of people, collectivist Marxism, or free-market Capitalism? Which system recognizes the individual's right to the property and wealth he or she has accumulated by trading the hours of their lives spent? Which system is voluntary, and doesn't rely upon force?

The Classical Liberal recognizes that the Progressives misunderstand the basic insights of economics: the law of supply and demand, and how to use the free-market mechanism to set the price voluntarily. Thus, the Progressives curse their economies with shortages, strife, bribery, corruption, bureaucracy, and a police state.

RESOURCES

Know Thy Enemies
IN DEFENSE OF MARXISM
http://www.marxist.com/
COMMUNIST PARTY USA
http://www.cpusa.org/

Know Thy Friends
FOUNDATION FOR ECONOMIC EDUCATION
http://fee.org/
INTERCOLLEGIATE STUDIES INSTITUTE
http://www.isi.org/

Chapter 2

Fiat Money and the Federal Reserve:
Printing "Funny Money" and Stagflation

PROGRESSIVES

When it comes to finance, Progressives are everywhere. They are in Democratic and Republican circles. They push an array of policies designed to empower government officials to manipulate everything about our money; particularly when it comes to its supply and value. Remember, the tell-tale sign of a Progressive is the goal of control. Characteristically, once Progressives get control of something, they want to be as free as possible to exercise that control. Call it the "Progressive Paradox."

Consider the Progressive approach to managing the United States dollar.

The dollar is still the world's premier currency. It is accepted in nearly every corner of the world as a medium of exchange. One would think the dollar's popularity would be linked to its value, which in turn would be tied to an independent commodity like gold. That notion is wrong. The dollar severed its last, frayed ties to a gold standard on August 5, 1971 after decades of increasing the ratio between dollars and gold. Why? Because Progressives on both sides of the political aisle want to enhance their power through the illusion of wealth creation.

Here's how it works. Progressives start by rejecting the idea of a gold standard because it fixes the amount of money in circulation to the amount of gold held in reserve. Thus, a gold standard "arbitrarily" restricts the amount of money in circulation. That, in turn, concentrates wealth in fewer hands because there are less dollars to go around. To Progressives, that's a problem because dollars equal wealth.

So for Progressives, the way to create more wealth is to create more dollars. Enter the Federal Reserve System. Unlike any other federal agency, the Fed exercises complete discretion in its decisions. It has no congressional oversight committee. It has never been audited. When the Fed decides to print more dollars, it does. And since the only guarantee of a dollar's value is the United States government's word, the printing of more money makes the United States taxpayers the ultimate guarantors of the Fed's print jobs.

That leads to problems. Big problems. Problems like a steadily devaluing dollar and inflation. Since dollars are worth less, the price of everything goes up. Eventually, people realize that more dollars in circulation do not equal more wealth..

CLASSICAL LIBERALS

Progressives promote the idea of a currency based on "trust." As always, the trust flows in one direction: from the people to their government. In America, the main form of currency is the dollar, the most recognizable – and popular – method of payment in the world. Yet the dollar itself is nothing more than a slice of paper and drizzles of ink. The only reason people use dollars is because they believe the government when it says dollars are valuable. It only works if people trust their government not to cheat them.

At times in our nation's history, paper money was backed by gold. That meant that for every dollar in circulation there was an equal amount of gold in a government vault. Most people carried gold (and silver) coins in their pockets. Few paper dollars were in circulation. People accepted dollars bills for payment instead of dollar gold coins because they trusted the government to just print only as much money as there was gold to support it, and the gold coins were always available to use instead.

Things change. There were pressures to get off the gold standard. Progressives like William Jennings Bryan led a populist movement called the "Silver Bugs" attempting to replace gold with the less valuable silver. The intended effect was to weaken the value of the dollar so that farmers owing money to banks could pay off their debts with cheaper money. Though Bryan was unsuccessful, industrialists like John D. Rockefeller and financiers like J.P. Morgan saw an opportunity to profit by weakening the gold standard.

Since the gold standard fixed the amount of dollars in circulation to the amount of gold held in government vaults, there was only a set number of dollars to be accumulated. In order to increase the supply of dollars – and, by extension, access to capital to expand their wealth – Rockefeller and Morgan instructed handpicked men to draft legislation at a resort on Georgia's Jekyll Island. Three years later, Progressive icon President Woodrow Wilson signed the legislation creating the Federal Reserve System in 1913.

At first, the Federal Reserve System (Fed) fixed the dollar to a gold standard, but not on a one-to-one rate. Instead, the Fed printed dollars in excess of government gold deposits, devaluing the money by creating more of it. The newly created paper money put more money in more people's hands, fueling the Roaring Twenties. Inflation, by definition, is simply an increase in the money supply. Inflation took over. It now took more dollars to buy the same products. But people felt rich. After all, look at their bank accounts – see all the dollars?

Then the Great Depression hit. In the 1920s, the private sector enjoyed the increased money supply, and spent it until some folks finally started requesting gold rather than paper. Knowing that the US Government had cheated the people, Progressive hero President Franklin D. Roosevelt's solution was to outlaw the people's gold coins. On April 3, 1933, people were forced to turn their gold over to the Federal Reserve Banks or face a 10 year jail term. Gold could only be used to balance the trading books between the US Government and foreign countries. During the 1930s, it was the federal government's turn to spend. Roosevelt increased both the paper money supply and government spending, which led to deficits and taxes, but no economic recovery. In fact, the stock market didn't reach its pre-1929 crash levels until 1954.

But people liked owning more dollars. It made them feel wealthy. To pay for the Vietnam War, in 1971, President Nixon – a Progressive Republican – reneged on America's promise to pay its bills to other countries in gold. Free from the last limits that gold imposed, the Fed undertook a vast new money printing exercise. The resulting inflation, combined with rising unemployment, create stagflation. Since then, the only guarantee backing the dollar's stated value is the word of the United States government. The Fed continues to print money at its whim, and declare its value: take it or leave it. Thus, the dollars we spend and accept today are products of fiat money; valuable only because the government says so.

For nearly 100 years, Americans trusted their government to provide a valuable money supply. So did the rest of the world. The greenback was "good as Gold". That trust has been repaid with policies that have replaced gold with Washington's say so.

Classical Liberals don't trust the government to do much of anything; especially when it comes to unilaterally deciding how much money to print, how high or low to set interest rates, and what value to declare the dollar. The only way to keep government honest is to remove its ability to devalue our money. That means returning to a full gold standard, as soon as possible, with a one-to-one correspondence of dollar bills in circulation to the actual amount of gold bullion stored in the vaults of the Government.

Better still, get out of the business of monopoly control of the most important commodity in the marketplace: the money. If you trust the marketplace, turn the supply of money back over to the private sector. That's what the Constitution envisions. And from 1776 through 1913 that's how America was successfully run. The US Government was limited to coining money authorized by Congress.

RESOURCES:

Know Thy Enemies

FEDERAL RESERVE

http://www.federalreserve.gov/

Know Thy Friends

LUDWIG VON MISES INSTITUTE

http://mises.org/

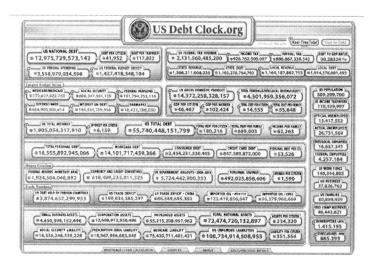

Chapter 3

Government Spending and Fiscal Deficits: "Legal" Ponzi Schemes and Bankruptcy

PROGRESSIVES

Perhaps you've heard the Progressive mantra that "it takes a village to raise a child" as a way to justify government intrusions into childrearing like public education. The phrase contains a kernel of every Progressive's received wisdom: each of us owes something to everyone else. Thanks to the New Deal, what's owed isn't just a moral obligation – it's a financial one too.

The Progressive rendering of American history explains one of the chief lessons they learned from the Great Depression: "we're all in this together." Society suffers when individuals are out of work and left destitute. But private charity and family support aren't enough to bridge the gap. Government is needed. Specifically, the federal government and programs like Social Security. Flush with money and a national reach, the feds can also enforce an agreement the common law disallowed: a perpetual contract.

The government calls this contract "generational" to make it sound nice. In reality, it is a perpetual generational wealth transfer from younger to older Americans. The Social Security taxes from workers immediately become the Social Security benefits to retirees. It is the definition of a Ponzi scheme. (More on that in the next section.)

Members of Generation X and Generation Y already figured this out. Problem is, they can't opt out or even "privatize" their Social Security account to invest in the stock market. Not only would that break the link between immediately turning taxes into benefits, it would also rob Progressives of the power to command and control the nation's largest "insurance" program.

Ask Progressives about the consensus that Social Security will be bankrupt before the current generation of workers retires, and they respond with emotional stories about the elderly losing their pensions if the current system is changed. Of course, the only way to balance the books is to either cut benefits or raise taxes, measures Progressives ridicule. It's more popular to spend on credit, and promise it will all work out in the future.

But the financial science is settled. Without drastic measures, Social

Security won't be solvent. Then again, that isn't the point for Progressives. All that matters is that we all feel connected to those before and after us – even if the feeling comes from the sensation of less money in our pockets for the future.

CLASSICAL LIBERALS

The New Deal brought a variety of innovations to the federal government, but perhaps none so enduring as the Social Security Administration. In the beginning, it was sold to older people as a way to provide money for them after they could no longer work. Younger workers were told that the level of income guaranteed under the program would entice their elders out of the labor market, thus freeing up jobs during the Great Depression. Everybody assumed that the money he or she paid into Social Security would be earmarked for their account. That was never the government's intent.

How could it be? In order to start a multi-generational social welfare program, the government needed money immediately to start paying older workers to get out of the labor market. Those people needed a guaranteed level of income to convince them not to work. And so began the practice of taxing current workers to pay the benefits of retirees.

In the financial world, paying older investors with money from newer investors is called a Ponzi scheme. The scheme takes its name from a once beloved businessman who implemented the model on a grandly ruinous scale. The system is fairly simple to run, and it can go on for years. Just ask now disgraced New York Ponzi scheme magician Bernie Madoff. For years analysts wondered how he could beat the market with consistently strong returns. Changes in the economy never seemed to affect Madoff's ability to produce great value for his clients. It was almost as if his annual pay-outs were mandated by law.

Now, we know better. If something sounds too good to be true, it almost always is. In the business world, models that don't work eventually get discovered, and the companies that use them fail. People lose their money. Most of the major business failures of the past decade occurred because companies' profits were based on fraud: Enron, WorldCom, and all the investment firms trading shady derivatives. Like today's dollar, there was no intrinsic value to the services these businesses provided; only the trust that investors gave them.

Consider the magic of Madoff. Many smart people couldn't explain his success; many more didn't care so long as they got a piece of it. Millions of Americans fall into the second group. They want to believe Progressives who say that Social Security will always be around to make good on its promise to pay. Surely, after forty years of paying into the system, something must be left over, right?

Not for younger workers. Though government mismanagement is the driving force behind Social Security's lack of funds, a key demographic reality is about to bring on a fiscal reckoning.

The Baby Boomer generation is retiring. As the largest generation in American history, it was responsible for the explosive growth in government tax receipts while members were working. In fact, they poured so much money into the treasury that President Lyndon Johnson took the historic increase and turned it into Medicare and Medicaid. More Ponzi schemes. Like Social Security, these entitlement programs grew. And grew. Since the Baby Boomers didn't replace themselves with an equal number of children, soon there will be more people retired than working.

There's an old adage that the best way to get out of a hole is to stop digging. Applied to our collapsing entitlement programs like Social Security, Medicare, and Medicaid, the best way to return fiscal sanity to the federal budget is to pair benefit levels to tax receipts. Better yet, eliminate the programs and the taxes that fund them so people can voluntarily invest in a financial model that actually works.

RESOURCES:

Know Thy Enemies

SOCIAL SECURITY ADMINISTRATION

http://www.ssa.gov/kids/workfacts.htm

Know Thy Friends

ARTICLE: The American Thinker: "The Social Security Ponzi Scheme"

http://www.americanthinker.com/2005/03/the_social_security_ponzi_sche.html

Chapter 4

Taxes and Over-regulation: Killing the Golden Goose of the Free Market or How to Create the New Mafia

PROGRESSIVES

Progressives believe that wealth beyond a certain amount is immoral. They, of course, decide the acceptable threshold. To correct this problem, Progressives conclude that people making more than the threshold must be forced to part with the "excess" amount of their wealth through coercion, commonly called taxation. Direct taxes come in the form of mandatory takings from income, sales, and purchases. Indirect taxes are fees for licenses, registrations, and other forms of compliance.

Both forms of taxation reduce the amount of wealth for individuals and society. The individual has less money to spend or invest in goods and services, which reduces the sales and thus the wealth of other members of society. In time, the overall economic output is less than what it could be. For Classical Liberals, this is the inevitable result of taxation. For Progressives, it is merely an effect of a moral economic policy.

To repeat, Progressives believe that wealth beyond a certain amount is immoral. According to the Obama Administration, income above $250,000 per year is the threshold of moral compensation. Treating higher income levels with harsher taxation rates is called "progressive" taxation, because the more you make, the more you pay in taxes as a percentage of your income.

Most people don't like to be discriminated against, whether the reason is based on race, gender, or economic status. Usually, if people are unable to get the government to act fairly, they resort to treating the law as a game with rules to be exploited. This is seen most clearly in filing income tax returns. Understandably, people want to pay as little in taxes as possible, so they use the rules in the tax code to minimize their income. Corporations act similarly. Their game is to structure compensation to avoid benefits being counted as taxable income.

At best, this means that people only appear to be making less than the governmentally approved threshold, with money left over to grow the economy. But since Progressives think they are entitled to other people's money, they eventually change the tax code making it impossible to avoid taxation. This leads to the worst scenario: people actually do make less than the threshold. That causes two results. First, there is an artificial cap on wealth. Second, the government takes in less money, emboldening it to lower the morally acceptable threshold to make up for the loss.

Over time, the market gets the hint. After a certain point, wealth is bad. But limiting wealth also limits productivity and entrepreneurship. Wages are depressed. Pretty soon, so are people. Industries contract, with many going extinct because of the lack of capital and a motivated labor force. Those that can outsource their jobs to countries where is it cheaper to do business.

And so the downward cycle continues until everyone is at the same income level. Taken to its logical conclusion, a Progressive's view of a moral economy policy is indistinguishable from Communism: from each according to their ability, to each according to their need. It makes perfect sense – just don't think about it too hard.

CLASSICAL LIBERALS

Classical liberals see wealth as potentially limitless, but the more it is taxed, the more limited it becomes. Therefore, in order to maximize wealth, it is necessary to minimize taxes.

Remember then Senator Obama's remark that progressive taxes on business owners like "Joe the Plumber" are good policy because it "spreads the wealth around"? That comment completes the Progressive belief that wealth above a certain level is immoral. After taking the excess away from higher earners, Progressives redistribute it to lower earners. This helps Progressives feel moral.

But there is another, far better, way to spread wealth around than through a government tax-and-spend system. Imagine an economy with no taxes. Every person gets to keep the money he earns. With his pockets swelling, he can then expand his neighbor's wealth by trading with her. She, in turn, would be able to do the same with another person, and so on down the line. In this kind of environment, each individual is empowered to increase society's wealth through free trade.

There is another benefit. Spending your own money makes you much more sensitive to the quality and cost of what you buy. The search for good value spurs businesses to offer choices. Consumers gravitate to the choices that best fit their sense of value, and the market shifts to accommodate their decisions. The driving forces behind this conversation between buyers and sellers are private individuals seeking to maximize their wealth while sharing it voluntarily with others.

There is no such conversation in a tax-and-spend system because the government chooses winners and losers without regard to market forces. The government does not demand the same level of value for its spending because the money it spends belongs to other people: taxpayers. Rather, because the money spent and the goods and services consumed are by other people, government agents have no incentive to demand top value for military jets, health care plans, or even janitorial service.

The key to spreading wealth is to create a system where individuals are only limited by their desire to work.

RESOURCES:

Know Thy Enemies

ECONOMIC POLICY INSTITUTE

http://www.epi.org/

COMMONWEAL INSTITUTE

http://www.commonwealinstitute.org/

Know Thy Friends

INSTITUTE FOR LIBERTY

http://www.instituteforliberty.org/index.php

COMPETITIVE ENTERPRISE INSTITUTE

http://cei.org/

Chapter 5

Census & Voting Fraud: Stealing Elections, the First Step Towards Totalitarianism

BACKGROUND

The United States Constitution requires the Federal Government to conduct a census of the American population every 10 years. The provision is found in Article I, Section 2: "[An] enumeration shall be made within three years after the first meeting of the Congress of the United States, and within every subsequent term of ten years, in such manner as they shall by law direct." The census is important because the numbers of citizens in each state determines the number of Congressional seats, Electoral College votes, and the amount of federal funding each state receives. If a mistake or an act of fraud were to occur, it would have national consequences. So, when it comes to the Census, it matters greatly how people are counted and who does the counting.

The same is true of an electoral system. In a democratic republic, a government's legitimacy is linked to the degree to which its elections are free, fair, and open. Moreover, since the 1960s, the Supreme Court has upheld the idea of "one man, one vote" as a cornerstone of electoral politics. The concern the doctrine tries to remedy is the intentional diluting of one group's votes by allocating equal representation to districts with substantially unequal populations. In such a system, the majority of voters are unable to elect a majority of representatives. At that time, the favored class was rural voters who blocked redistricting for decades to hinder urban areas from getting their share of representatives. Today, popular majority representation is still under attack. Now, it's in the form of voting fraud where operatives falsify voter registrations, absentee ballots, and duplicate votes to enrich a turnout that doesn't exist.

PROGRESSIVES

Progressives know that one of the best ways to gain support for their ends is to falsely claim the use of Classical Liberal means. For example, if the Government must do something yet lacks the resources to do it, a private enterprise should be contracted to complete the task. Enter the Association of Community Organizations for Reform Now (ACORN)! Since the Census Bureau usually contracts with staffing agencies to fill the once-a-decade workload, why not use a non-profit with years of experience in getting information? One reason not to do it is because ACORN is under criminal investigation in several states for a litany of voter registration fraud allegations. Another reason is that several of its local affiliates were caught on camera advising undercover reporters how to skirt the law to set up a prostitution ring. The latter reason finally caused the Census Bureau to sever its ties with ACORN.

While the severance with ACORN helped alleviate the mounting likelihood of Census fraud, it did not eradicate the main cause. At the center of the Progressive agenda for the Census is intentionally distorting the population count. The easiest way to do this is to deliberately not ask whether a person is a citizen or legal resident. This omission skews the data collection so that some sub-populations are over-represented. That in turn benefits the groups that gain money and political power from counting such groups in larger numbers.

It's a straight-forward way to buy votes. In the fall of 2009, the White House transferred the control of directing the 2010 Census from the Commerce Department to the White House itself. The Progressives in control of the political machinery of the White House now have the ability to count exactly whom they please - and who will most benefit the Progressives in the five national elections over the next 10 years.

The primary beneficiaries of this new "don't ask, don't tell" policy are illegal immigrant populations and Democratic politicians. Illegal immigrants benefit because they are counted the same as citizens and legal residents. Democratic politicians benefit because they cater to illegal immigrant communities. The result is a greater number of congressional seats apportioned to states with high numbers of illegal immigrants. Thus, even though illegal immigrants do not have a right to vote, they have the "right" to be represented. This shifts the real voting power in Congress from states with law-abiding citizens to states with more law-breaking people who are generally more dependent on the welfare benefits provided by government.

Even more troubling, Progressives believe illegal immigrants do have the right to vote, by simply being in the United States. That's why Progressives oppose policies like Voter ID which require a person to produce a valid, Government-issued identification card before voting. Government-ID cards can only be issued to citizens or legal residents. The card helps prove residency in the district and citizenship or legal residency status.

Of course, Progressives claim that eliminating the citizen or legal resident question from the Census Questionnaire eliminates supposed racism, bigotry, and harassment from the data collection. It follows – for them – that the same is true when voting. If people are asked to verify their citizenship or residency status, they will feel harassed and be afraid to vote. In essence, the Progressive argument is that in order to increase Census responses and voter turnout, the Government should not ask whether the people participating are actually Americans. Never mind that removing this baseline qualification corrupts both the Census and our elections by letting foreign nationals determine states' congressional seats and occupants. If Progressives can't represent a majority of Americans citizens and legal residents, they'll expand the Census and Voting Rolls until they get a majority that they can represent..

And it's all brought to you at taxpayer expense, courtesy of the Obama White House.

CLASSICAL LIBERALS

The best way to ensure that the Census reflects citizens and legal residents is to reduce the number of illegal immigrants. Since the Fourteenth Amendment requires the federal Government to count "the whole number of persons" in a state, illegal immigrants must be counted in the Census. When coupled with the requirement in Article I, Section 2, that congressional apportionment must be based on the number of people counted, the result creates a perverse incentive to expand the flow of illegal immigration into the country to dilute the voting power of lawful citizens and legal residents.

These outcomes – skewed congressional apportionment and diluted voting power – are two of the biggest motivators for Progressives opposing stricter enforcement of American immigration laws. Once here, Progressives encourage illegal immigrants to vote in elections. When governments attempt to pass minimal identification requirements prior to voting, Progressives cry foul. How dare Americans try to make would-be voters prove they actually live in the district in which they want to vote? In fact, it took a Supreme Court decision upholding an Indiana Voter ID law to quell Progressive opponents.

The law at issue was controversial only if you think requiring a US-issued photo ID prior to voting is tantamount to racial or socio-economic discrimination. Though that's the public stance of Progressives, as discussed above, it's hardly the real reason. Like Classical Liberals, they clearly know that the best solution for cleaning up the corruption in voting is to require photo identification before casting a ballot. Anything else allows people to game the system. Only by requiring photo ID plus a name and address check of the voter rolls can election workers ensure that the person standing in front of them is actually qualified to vote. Until then, Progressives will continue to steal elections. And paid stooges will be able to vote a dozen or more times in the same election under different names in different precincts. Just like in the good ol' days of the Chicago machine run by "Boss" Richard J. Daley.

Another way to commit voter fraud is to sign up for vote-by-mail and absentee ballots, increasingly popular with voters. It's easy to jimmy the system to steal the vote of a real voter, or recently deceased citizen. John Fund, Wall Street Journal columnist has written *Stealing Elections: How Voter Fraud Threatens Our Democracy*, the definitive how-to book on corruption - with lots of real life examples.

As Fund points out, by 2001 in many American cities, more people were registered to vote than the US Census listed as the total number of residents over 18! In 1999, CBS' 60 Minutes found people in California who used the mail-in forms to register pets and make-believe people to vote - and it worked. The illegal Mexican alien who assassinated the Mexican presidential candidate Luis Donaldo Colosio was illegally registered to vote in San Pedro, L.A. County - twice!

RESOURCES:

Know Thy Enemies

ASSOCIATION OF COMMUNITY ORGANIZATIONS FOR REFORM NOW (ACORN)

http://www.acorn.org

PROJECT VOTE

http://www.projectvote.org

Know Thy Friends

ARTICLE: The 2010 Census, the Constitution and You (Accuracy in Media)

www.aim.org/guest-column/the-2010-census-the-constitution-and-you

ARTICLE: Democracy Imperiled: America's election problems (National Review Online)

www.nationalreview.com/comment/fund200409130633.asp

Chapter 6

Political Corruption in the Government & the Marketplace: The Chicago Mob Rule

PROGRESSIVES

Progressives argue that we all pay a terrible price when crony capitalism infects our political system. The practice of doling out government contracts to favored business interests usually results in taxpayers paying far more than they otherwise would. That is particularly true when government contracts are awarded without accepting bids from competitors. The most recent Bush Administration was expert at giving away no-bid contracts to friendly businesses during the Iraq occupation.

In many ways, crony capitalism is another kind of corporate welfare. For all the talk about letting the free market decide winners and losers, many businesses are more than happy to shuck the uncertainties of open competition for the peace of mind brought about by a backroom, sweetheart political deal. This kind of hypocrisy shows that the private sector is just a smokescreen for wealthy people to hide behind when it suits them. The rest of the time, they are trying to stick it to the taxpayer while laughing all the way to their off-shore bank accounts.

CLASSICAL LIBERALS

Classical Liberals *always* oppose distorting processes and markets to privilege those who would not succeed in a free competition. Moreover, Classical Liberals share Progressives' disgust for politicians who enact pro-business – rather than pro-market – policies that benefit a particular business or industry at the expense of competitors. However, Progressives aren't willing to generalize the principle. Rather, they want to decry pro-business *largesse* while lining the pockets of labor unions.

It takes a coalition to get elected. Since the Government exercises the power to tax, regulate, and subsidize, many people are drawn towards campaigns to build a relationship with a politician who might be able to help them down the road. Like most things, both the kind and degree of help given determine whether it should be labeled corruption.

"Machine" politics definitely qualify. A political machine is an informal organization of people working to produce electoral victories in exchange for Government jobs or contracts. As a matter of historical fact, almost all American political machines are run by Democrats. The reason being Democrats have a key advantage over Republicans when it comes to staffing a machine: labor union members. The point of a union is to reward members through collective bargaining. Support the leadership and they will take care of you. Thus, since union members are conditioned to expect a *quid quo pro* relationship from higher-ups, it's easy to translate that arrangement into Government jobs and contracts when a Democratic candidate gets elected.

That is the key to the Daley Machine's grip on power in Chicago. Graduates of the machine include several Obama Administration officials including White House Chief of Staff Rahm Emmanuel, and Senior Advisors Valerie Jarrett and David Axelrod. During then Senator Barack Obama's presidential campaign, labor unions like the Service Employees Union (SEIU) were critical to advancing his candidacy. Now, President Obama and his inner circle are setting up the machine model on a national scale.

White House records show that SEIU chief Andy Stern was the most frequent visitor during President Obama's first year in office. Stern's influence was felt in California when his representatives pressured state officials not to cut funding for a program employing union members. His fingerprints touched every version of the Democrats' health care reform process, at every turn seeking to protect union compensation. The agreement to exempt union contracts from a tax on so-called "Cadillac" health plans is an example of Stern getting a better deal from the Government than anyone else.

That is the essence of crony capitalism; the only difference is the Government is favoring labor unions instead of business interests. What makes this kind of distortion worse is the repeatable nature of the exchange. The unions like SEIU that feed vote counts can also be employed to disrupt Tea Party rallies, silence town hall participants, and protest whatever entity is labeled on opponent of Obama's Progressive agenda. That kind of continual work will rack up a lot of billable hours for unions to collect. As we've this past year with the auto bailouts, stimulus package, and health care bill, Progressives in the Government know where to send the check.

RESOURCES:

Know Thy Enemies

THE SERVICE EMPLOYEES INTERNATIONAL UNION

http://www.seiu.org/index.php

Know Thy Friends

ARTICLE: Unholy Union: Why is the SEIU boss the White House's most frequent visitor?

http://nrd.nationalreview.com/article/?q=ZGFmMDY4NzdkMmIwZTQ1M zU2ZDA4NGZhNzJlNGU2MTE=

Chapter 7

Media Bias and Distortion. The Dirty Secret: Why the Main Stream Media is Hemorrhaging Viewers & Readers

PROGRESSIVES

Progressives will tell you its all capitalism's fault. An unregulated internet coupled with independent bloggers willing to create free content are what's killing traditional news outlets like newspapers and broadcast networks. The mainstream media (MSM) simply can't compete with partisan ideologues who abandon the pay-to-read model. Their solutions range from government bailouts to cracking down on dissenting opinions by re-instituting the "fairness doctrine". To modify an old saying, if you can't beat them, get the Government to regulate them out of existence.

In their most delusional incarnation, MSM defenders claim that the real cause of their demise is the deliberate slanting of news to fit a certain point of view. Fox News, Matt Drudge, Andrew Breitbart, along with the legion of conservative and libertarian bloggers violate every canon of journalistic ethics by inserting themselves into the story to report their opinions as facts. Progressives claim these entities play on people's emotions to distract viewers and readers from the cruel light of reason. Moreover, replacing an objective search for the truth with the profit motive commercializes news in a way that undermines the intrepid journalist's role as educator. The result is a provider-customer relationship that rewards giving people what they want instead of telling them what they need to hear.

If those lines of reasoning sound paternalistic, they are. The MSM has been hemorrhaging viewers and readers for decades because members refuse to recognize that they are in the news business, not the news aristocracy. In a way, though, a certain sense of elitism is understandable. Most of the people working in news rooms, magazine shops, and television studios were trained to think of themselves as enlightened gatekeepers of knowledge. Here again is the Progressive conceit: power over other people's lives. Blessed with journalism degrees from Columbia, Northwestern, Missouri, Syracuse, or California, graduates trade one set of Progressive mentors for another when they enter the MSM job market. There they learn to echo the talking points handed down from the Columbia Journalism Review and disseminated by former students-turned-editors.

All was working well until the explosion of conservative talk radio. Finally, news consumers had an alternative to the MSM's monolithic consensus about the world. When people were given a choice, they exercised it. The same thing happened with the arrival of the internet. In the mid-1990s, Fox News began to assert itself as a conservative alternative to the ABC-NBC-CBS axis. Characteristically, Progressives interpret the rise of conservative and libertarian presentations of news as a failure of deregulation. During Ronald Reagan's presidency, free speech supporters successfully ended the Federal Communications Commission's "fairness doctrine" – a federal rule requiring broadcasters to air all sides of a controversial issue. In practice, the rule was used by   White Houses of both parties to stifle dissent by threatening to strip stations of their broadcast license. Additionally, the arbitrary nature of the enforcement led many stations not to air deliberate one side versus the other commentaries. Instead, they embedded their viewpoints in their news coverage. When the rule was rescinded, the practice remained.

Now, Progressives want to reinstate the fairness doctrine with the expectation that it will destroy conservative talk radio and substantially impair Fox News. True, it might also shut down MSNBC's overtly liberal bias, but it, like the now defunct liberal talk radio network Air America, is an unprofitable, Progressive-subsidized platform for extreme leftist views. Those casualties are acceptable collateral damage in the Progressives' drive to get back to being the only voice in the public square. Like other dictatorial propagandists, the MSM realizes that sometimes you have to sacrifice a few friends for the good of the movement. After all, free speech doesn't pay.

CLASSICAL LIBERALS

The causes of the problems facing the MSM are easy for a Classical Liberal to see. The first problem is that the Progressives running the MSM refuse to acknowledge that they are in the news business. A business thrives when it finds a need in its market and fills it. Part of seeing a business opportunity is identifying a customer base and respecting its desires. The MSM doesn't respect its readers and viewers. At best, it sees them as either in enlightened agreement or unsophisticated denial. From the Tea Party movement to ClimateGate, and Sarah Palin to Glenn Beck, the Progressive elites who program the news are seemingly incapable of covering differing points of view with anything other than contempt. They fail to recognize that the millions of people watching and reading conservative and libertarian alternatives are of a different opinion than they. For that, these millions get ridiculed. People don't pay for that kind of harassment. Instead, they take their dollars to other news sources.

Those motivations explain the on-camera and in-print talents' audience-shrinking bias, but it doesn't explain the larger reason why many MSM outlets support Progressive candidates and causes. For that, one has to look further up the food chain. The reality for all broadcast networks and most newspapers is that they are owned by major corporations whose primary commercial interest is not news. Much like the MSM's preoccupation with using government regulations like the fairness doctrine to stamp out competition, companies like General Electric (GE) who own NBC (pending a sale to Comcast) have an insatiable hunger for government contracts. When billions of dollars are at stake, corporate heavyweights are not shy about using their news and entertainment operations to promote policies that will benefit them come contracting time.

The most recent example is GE's enthusiastic support for the Obama Administration's first stimulus package and health care reform. At first blush, it may seem that a major corporation like GE couldn't possibly support legislation that will result in higher taxes. What about their bottom line? Actually, GE knows the way Progressives think and is well positioned to take advantage of their policies. It supports stimulus spending because much of it went to "green jobs" and "infrastructure" projects – just the kind GE specializes in with its energy efficiency and health IT lines of business.

Under Obama's stimulus priorities, GE stands to gain millions in government subsidies. The same is true for its health-related technology ventures. So, in an effort to prove its Progressive bona fides, NBC co-opted several of its entertainment and news productions to promote a greener, healthier world during November 2009. The show "30 Rock" gave a cameo to Al Gore, while "The Office," "Heroes," and "The Biggest Loser" all incorporated environmental themes into their storylines. The news side was tasked with issuing special reports on environmental issues. With all this direction, it is little wonder "NBC Nightly News" took over a week to report on the ClimateGate data destruction conspiracy that was swirling around the internet.

For the most part, corporate executives don't have to push too hard to get their journalists to report favorably on Progressives and their policies. If the parent company can get rich while allowing its reporters and anchors to promote larger government involvement in the environment, health care, and energy, doesn't everybody win? That is, everybody, except the viewers at home, of course.

If you are reading this book, you've at least had a feeling that something wasn't right with traditional news outlets. You knew something was wrong when the business community representatives at Obama's "jobs summit" were CEOs of multi-national corporations – not small business owners. The problem is more than just an incestuous Progressive family tree with branches in academia, the MSM, and non-profits. It's the empowering of these people by business elites who use the Progressive mania for higher taxes and more spending to enrich their companies and themselves. Remember, businesses don't pay taxes, individuals do. Unless, of course, you're wealthy enough to know the right accountant.

RESOURCES:

Know Thy Enemies

*Nearly all major metropolitan newspapers, and television networks – view responsibly

Know Thy Friends

ARTICLE: Back to Muzak? Congress and the Un-Fairness Doctrine (Heritage Foundation)

http://www.heritage.org/Research/Regulation/wm1472.cfm

ARTICLE: NBC's ObamaVision: GE Uses Network to Push Obama's Green Agenda – And Rakes in the Dough (Big Hollywood)

http://bighollywood.breitbart.com/bshapiro/2009/11/16/propaganda-ge-uses-nbc-to-push-obamas-green-agenda-and-rakes-in-the-dough/

ANDREW BREITBART'S BIG JOURNALISM

http://bigjournalism.com/

Chapter 8

Freedom of the Press: Government Intrusion, Censorship & Control Over What You Read and What You Think

PROGRESSIVES

Some people can't be trusted to tell the truth. For Progressives, that maxim applies to journalists and institutions that deviate from Progressive orthodoxy. Combating such heretics employs a strategy that alternates between ridiculing them as incompetent and charging them as deliberate liars. The cumulative effect eventually marginalizes dissenters, and acts as a warning to their sympathizers.

To a certain extent, that kind of sharp dealing can lead to investigative reporting that bears out the truth or falsity of such allegations, but only if the mudslinging is conducted between members of a free press. A major problem arises, however, when sustained attacks come not from the private sector, but from the Government.

As discussed before, Progressives do not distinguish between the public and private sectors because for them, everything is political. Everything is about gaining, using, and retaining power. If a personally satisfying motive can be best fulfilled through the aegis of government, so be it. Progressive participation in corporate welfare is one example. Turning the prestige of high government office against private sector opponents is another.

A recent example is the Obama Administration's targeting of Fox News for its critical coverage. In addition to banning White House personnel from appearing on the network, Obama senior management threatened fellow Democrats. If any Democratic politician or strategist appeared on the network during the White House-imposed blackout period, Team Obama would punish them at the next opportunity.

After a time, the ban was lifted. But that isn't how a Progressive media marginalization campaign typically operates. Usually, the Progressive-controlled Government declares war on a dissenting news outlet in an effort to cow it into submission or run it out of business.

In South America, Progressives like Venezuela's Hugo Chavez have perfected the process of exterminating free media. The Government and its cronies start by directly attacking the outlet's objectivity, and move swiftly to accuse it of lying. Soon, the Government claims the outlet is a public danger, further marginalizing it by scaring away advertisers and public supporters. Finally, the Government silences the outlet by revoking its license, banning its existence or nationalizing its operation. If the latter, the once independent outlet becomes just another mouthpiece for the Progressive regime.

The death of an independent opposition leads to distorted news and a consensus slanted in favor of the ruling elites. This allows Progressives inside and outside the Government to operate freely in public re-education campaigns designed to build support for Progressive policies. In effect, the freedom of the press becomes the freedom to say anything in line with Progressive orthodoxy. But that's not so bad; right? After all, if Progressives tell the truth, why do you need someone spreading lies?

CLASSICAL LIBERALS

A free and energetic press is essential to the preservation of a free people. The Founding Fathers knew that in a democracy many conflicting opinions would arise, and that the best way to distinguish the wheat from the chaff would be to let individual citizens decide. James Madison is famous for expressing this sentiment regarding the need to keep government out of religion. The same thinking holds true for information about the Government itself.

All governments are criticized. Some criticisms are based in fact; others are the product of purely ideological differences. Whichever the case, the freedom of the press as guaranteed in the First Amendment to the United States Constitution means nothing if it fails to protect the freedom to criticize the Government. This is true for one simple reason: if people are not allowed to think and speak critically about their government, they will be unable to strengthen its weaknesses, or correct its abuses.

The press is more than the corporate media giants that dominate newsstands and television channels. The press – especially the free press – is made up of every blogger, reporter, letter-to-the editor writer, and self-publisher contributing content to the information market. At its core, the press is every individual with an opinion or fact that wants to share it. No one has a right to force his views on other people, nor does he have the right to force a news outlet to publish them. All freedom-respecting people understand this. The danger in today's politicized media environment, though, is forcing certain opinions out of the public square because they conflict with the Progressive worldview.

Consider the dramatically different reactions from Progressives and Classical Liberals to perceived bias in news reporting. In the 1980s, people concerned with the overtly liberal slant to news coverage founded the Media Research Center (MRC). MRC studies the causes and effects of media bias. Since then, other entities have become expert in showing how stories are crafted to advance a Progressive ideology. These entities are in the business of investigative reporting, and their business is booming.

Supposedly, Progressives tried to copy this model with groups like Media Matters for America; a watchdog organization with the stated purpose to ferret out conservative media bias. Of course, reading the Media Matters website it becomes instantly clear that the group is merely an arm of the Progressive movement. A recent example is the aggressive pro-public option internet commercial it ran featuring actress Heather Graham. By doing this, Media Matters went beyond exposing bias, and jumped into the fray as a fellow participant. That is their right, but it shows how shallow are Progressive claims to be anything other than an advocate for statist policies.

The truth has nothing to fear from a free and frank debate about it. In a free society, there will be many false prophets competing with honest men and women for support. All should be allowed to make their case, and subject them arguments to a vigorous examination. Such an examination is impossible without an energetic press free to follow the facts wherever they go so that we the people will not be led astray. It is in this context that Classical Liberals unequivocally support the freedom of the press because when the truth is found, it will set us all free.

RESOURCES:

Know Thy Enemies
MEDIA MATTERS
http://mediamatters.org/

Know Thy Friends
MEDIA RESEARCH CENTER
http://www.mrc.org/public/default.aspx
NEWSBUSTERS
http://newsbusters.org/

Chapter 9

Loss of Personal Privacy: The Rise of Big Brother Watching Everyone All the Time

PROGRESSIVES

Today, we live in a dramatically interconnected world. The mix of free trade, easy international travel, and government spending gives both public and private actors an interest in protecting our global system. When it comes to maintaining our quality of life, the name of the game is preempting threats to our security, our economy, and our personal well-being. Acknowledging this reality, it becomes apparent that government must have a role in monitoring individuals in order to protect society. As we've seen with the 9/11 terrorist attacks and the Wall Street-inspired financial meltdown, the old adage is true: it only takes a few bad apples to spoil the whole bunch. Though mindful of privacy concerns, it is nonetheless necessary to enhance government's ability to react quickly when it senses a threat to our country.

There is no better recent example than the 9/11 terrorist attacks. They could have been stopped. But local, state, and federal law enforcement agencies were not coordinated well enough to share their information and connect the dots before the nineteen hijackers boarded their planes. There is more. Prior to that day, law enforcement officials faced an even bigger obstacle to preemption: lack of authority to monitor the activities of terrorists inside America. That changed with the passage of the USA PATRIOT Act. Now, our security system has many of the tools it needs to stop a terrorist before he acts. The 9/11 attacks are an event that should never be repeated. The USA PATRIOT Act makes that commitment possible.

There are other threats inside our country as well. Each of them lowers the standard of living for the majority of Americans by creating unnecessary risks to our health, safety, and financial integrity. A few examples are people who drive while talking on a cell phone, smoke in a public space, and choose an unhealthy lifestyle that saddles others with the bill. If we are ever going to get a handle on senseless deaths and wasteful government spending, these are the kinds of activities that need to be eradicated from our society. We can't afford to let a reckless few ruin our health and wealth.

But we can't afford to physically monitor every destructive behavior, either. The cost in manpower would be too great when considered alongside government's other commitments. Thankfully, the British people found a silver budget bullet to solve this problem: more cameras, less cops. As of 2006, England had 4.2 million closed circuit television (CCTV) cameras mounted in public spaces. That comes out to one camera for every 14 people in the country. With government spending on the upswing, the Home Office (responsible for domestic policy) is now allocating up 78% of its police budget to camera technology. This means that England can spend less on human police staff for expenses like health care, time off, and raises.

Surveillance technology has other benefits aside from reducing crime. These include using GPS monitors in automobiles to pinpoint motorists in distress; greater sharing of internet activity to help advertisers target consumers; and cataloguing key strokes on company computers to gauge worker output. All of these protocols have been enormously successful in keeping government – and even businesses – informed.

The key to making our security, economy, and personal well-being more efficient are more protected is to learn from our mistakes. Bad people can exploit gaps in a system that does not control for behavior that harms the community. We seem to learn that lesson every time an unaccountable group wrecks havoc; be they terrorists on airplanes or financiers on the housing market. Sometimes, we all have to give up a little anonymity in order to regain our right to be free from fear.

CLASSICAL LIBERALS

When deciding between competing policy concerns, it is prudent to judge them in light of the fundamental law of our nation: the United States Constitution and its amendments. The Ninth Amendment guarantees that "The enumeration in the Constitution, of certain rights, shall not be construed to deny or disparage others retained by the people." That means that the failure of a certain right to be included in either the Constitution or its amendments does not imply that the right is not held by the people. Put another way, we the people enjoy rights that are not specifically mentioned in the Constitution and its amendments. The Ninth Amendment says so.

One of the best ways to determine whether an un-enumerated right is covered by the Ninth Amendment is to see whether it can be implied from other, enumerated rights. The right to privacy falls into this category. While it is not individually mentioned, it can be implied from several of the amendments in the Bill of Rights. For example, the Third Amendment prohibits government from quartering soldiers in private homes. The Fourth Amendment prohibits government from searching and seizing individuals and their property, unless holding a warrant supported by probable cause. The Fifth Amendment prohibits the government from coercing an individual to incriminate himself.

The principle tying these amendments together is an implied right to privacy. It is to protect a homeowner's privacy that government is not allowed to force a citizen to bed and board its military. It is to protect a person's privacy that government is not allowed to search and seize her private property without reasonable cause and a sworn warrant. And it is to protect the privacy of the accused that government is not allowed to compel a confession, whether in the station house or on the witness stand.

When read together, the first eight amendments in the Bill of Rights reads like what they are: specific limitations on the power of government. But as the Ninth Amendment makes clear, the rights of we the people don't stop with just eight. As a general rule, government is not entitled to know the thoughts or acts of American citizens. This means that our government does not have the right to monitor us in the hopes of preempting bad behavior. Especially when the behavior to be preempted pertains to the foods we eat, the websites we visit, or the views we hold.

Progressives cannot accept this. Ever the power-grabbing opportunists, they know that Americans do not support creating a Nanny State for its own sake. So, Progressives construct their policies, draft their laws, and wait for a catastrophic event to implement them. While some Progressives howled at passage of the USA PATRIOT Act, others quietly supported it and waited for an opportunity to expand government's national security power grab into a domestic monitoring network. They helped condition people to increased surveillance by pushing intrusive measures like fines for smoking, bans on cell phone usage while driving, and penalties for selling or buying food with trans fat.

The starkest example of the increase in the surveillance state is the unrelenting Progressive push for "red light" cameras at stop lights. The policy was sold as a way to reduce police presence while ratcheting up enforcement. Heard that rationale before? Once the surveillance infrastructure is in place, it will be a small adjustment to turn a camera taking snapshots into one sending a live feed to a monitoring station. Maybe they already do. It's not that easy to tell the difference.

But if a person has nothing to hide, he has nothing to fear; right? Wrong. Think about the last time you were in an elevator talking with someone, and a stranger got on. You stopped talking to your friend until the stranger, or you two, exited. You did that not because you probably had something to hide. You did it because you wanted privacy when faced with someone you don't know. A private citizen doesn't have the right to know your thoughts, actions, or associations. Neither does the government.

RESOURCES:

Know Thy Enemies

ARTICLE: *Britain is 'surveillance state'*

http://news.bbc.co.uk/2/hi/uk/6108496.stm

ARTICLE: *'Talking' CCTV scolds offenders (BBC News)*

http://news.bbc.co.uk/2/hi/uk_news/england/6524495.stm

ARTICLE: *Britons Weary of Surveillance in Minor Cases (New York Times)*

http://www.nytimes.com/2009/10/25/world/europe/25surveillance.html?_r=3&pagewanted=1&hp

ARTICLE: *Surveillance State (The American Conservative)*

http://www.amconmag.com/article/2003/may/19/00008/

Know Thy Friends

ELECTRONIC FRONTIER FOUNDATION

http://www.eff.org/

ELECTRONIC PRIVACY INFORMATION CENTER

http://epic.org/

THE SURVEILLANCE STUDIES NETWORK

http://www.surveillance-studies.net/

Chapter 10

Education in the Government Schools:
Dumbing Down America's Youth

PROGRESSIVES

If you listen to a Progressive talk about K-12 education, you're likely to think that the most important problems facing public education are meeting the needs of particular groups. Foreign students need more training in their native language. Minority students need more assistance in improving standardized test scores and graduation rates. Special needs students need more access to programs that help them overcome their handicaps. Administrators need more money for staff to measure and resource student performance. And then there are unionized teachers. They need more money, less students, and quicker tenure.

These groups are powerful voices in the arena of public education because they have teams of advocates in law firms, the media, organized labor, and government bureaucracies – all card-carrying institutions of the Progressive movement. Since the people controlling public education funding are politicians, almost all of the advocates' attention is focused on increasing local, state, and federal spending to benefit the groups mentioned above. More spending leads to one of two consequences: higher taxes or higher deficits.

But for these groups, the costs are worth it. They always are. And what do taxpayers get for the increased "investments" in education? Since World War II, a halving of America's literacy rate, innumerable regulations creating teacher and student "rights", and a dramatic increase in the number of graduates who need remedial education upon entering college. The cure, according to Progressives, is more money and more rules. More "oversight" and more "accountability" are always the solutions to the problems.

But the only way to achieve these goals is to spend more taxpayer money. Money equals powers. And since the core of Progressive philosophy is to increase the role of the State, the more Government funds education, the more education becomes a Government-directed enterprise. Take, for example, No Child Left Behind, the landmark federal legislation that dramatically increased the Federal Government's role in local K-12 schools. With every dollar that flows from Washington, D.C., to a school district near you, the Department of Education's ability to determine success grows. Progressives involved in education support this. To them, it doesn't matter which level of government calls the shots so long as Progressive members can influence the direction.

Remember, Progressives want power. Power is relative, so in order to have power, there must be another who does not. In K-12 public education, the powerful are the unions, attorneys, and bureaucrats who make policy. Under the system they have created, students and their parents are the ones shouldering the burdens of spending more and learning less.

CLASSICAL LIBERALS

Focusing exclusively on traditionally government funded schools is not the kind of comprehensive solution needed to cure what ails our nation's K-12 system. While it's true that proposals like teacher merit pay, distance-learning via computers, and standardized testing are all worthwhile to pursue for these types of schools, it is even more important to remember that they are only one part of a much larger education market. Other types of schools – both public and private – should be included in policy discussions because the main goal of education policy should be to educate as many students as best as possible. Defining "best" should be left to the parents of students, and the only way they can choose what's best is to have a choice between all the types of schools in the education market place.

The first place to start if looking for an alternative to traditional public schools is to consider alternative public schools – i.e. charter schools. Some of the best charter school laws are in places with the worst public school systems. (E.g. Washington, D.C., and California) Charter schools give parents a publically-funded school without unionized teachers and staff, statisticians masquerading as administrators, or curriculum requirements mandated by Progressives. Instead, they get innovative educators free to accomplish the goals of public education: graduates who can read, write, think, speak, and compute at their grade level.

Another choice that should be available to parents is using the amount of yearly per pupil spending allocated for their child as a voucher redeemable at a private school. Similar to state and federal loans to students at private colleges and universities, a K-12 voucher would enable parents to choose educational environments that best fit their families. The schools may be secular or sectarian, but since the primary goal of education policy is to educate every student as best as possible, like college, the best possible education for a particular student may come at a private school. That should be welcome news to state and local budget writers because for every student enrolled at a non-government school, there is one less desk, parking space, uniform, or lunch that must be provided. When aggregated, larger private school enrollments lead to less staff, buildings, and campuses that need constructing and maintaining.

Finally, parents should be able to keep their education tax dollars and apply them towards homeschooling their children. They could use a model similar to a Health Savings Account, and call it an Education Savings Account. Money would be put in a special, tax-free account and spent on the child's education expenses: textbooks, supplies, field trips, and the like.

For classical liberals, the possibilities are endless. The logic of free markets means that entrepreneurs in every field – even education – will be rewarded for producing a quality product at an affordable price. It may not be possible to get the Government out of the education industry. But it is impractical to act as though traditional public schools are (or should be) the only players in the education market. People want choices because they breed competition and provide alternatives. That was the logic the Founding Fathers followed in disestablishing religion. If the idea works in the most important arena of human existence, why not in the education of the next generation?

RESOURCES:

Know Thy Enemies
NATIONAL EDUCATION ASSOCIATION
http://www.nea.org/

Know Thy Friends
HEARTLAND INSTITUTE
http://www.heartland.org/suites/education/
HERITAGE FOUNDATION
http://www.heritage.org/research/Education/bg2179.cfm

Chapter 11

Illegal Immigration vs. Legal Immigration: Honest Future Citizens vs. Sneaking in the Back Door

No other issue speaks more clearly to the debate about what it means to be an American than immigration. There are two kinds of immigration: legal and illegal. What makes an immigrant legal is complying with the rules and regulations for coming to and staying in the United States of America. Not complying with those rules and regulations, and yet coming and staying anyway in the country is illegal. Yes, the laws are cumbersome and the process should be simplified to better serve the people being regulated. But this is, after all, the federal government we're talking about. Despite the difficulty of the tax code, taxpayers are still responsible for following it. If they don't, the IRS will take notice. Why should ICE be any different?

PROGRESSIVES

Progressives don't think this way. They don't argue for changing the regulations they don't like – or even getting rid of them. Instead, they want to create more laws. If the current immigration system is too complicated or too easy to flout, then just ignore it. That's why they advocate giving illegal immigrants legal status through a one-size-fits-all amnesty. So long as a person is in the country illegally, he can become an American citizen. No waiting in lines. No filling out paperwork. No comprehensive background check. If you managed to slip past border security and the local police, you are home free!

Look at the history of immigration "reform" beginning with Senator Ted Kennedy' immigration bill in 1965. It eliminated the quota system for admission, and its preference for immigrants from Western Europe. Later he spearheaded the landmark 1986 amnesty bill granting American citizenship to 2.7 million illegal aliens. In 2006 and 2007, Kennedy was once again trying to force a bill through Congress that would give amnesty to millions more illegal immigrants. In every instance Kennedy and the Democratic caucus followed a two-step model. First, call anyone who supports border enforcement a racist hostile to America's heritage as an immigrant destination. Then, argue that it is too difficult to police and punish the illegal immigrants already here, so the best course of action is to grant them amnesty.

The reason for supporting lax border enforcement followed by amnesty is simple: Progressives believe that the vast majority of newly legalized immigrants would support their policies and candidates. In this way, amnesty is really just a giant voter registration sign-up sheet. Get a Social Security Number and vote progressive! Why do Progressives think most of the newly made Americans would vote for them? Because illegal immigrants have already shown that they are comfortable with disregarding the law to advance their self-interest. And that's the hallmark of Progressivism!

When Progressives look at illegal immigrants, they see voters because they see dependents. It's true, illegal immigrants are "in the shadows" because they cannot live fully free and open lives. Progressives like it that way because it makes illegal immigrants dependent on Progressives as their advocates inside and outside the government. Progressives control the non-profit groups and law firms that represent illegal immigrants before deportation committees, judges, and employers. And in exchange for this representation and a generational amnesty bill, Progressives expect illegal immigrants-turned-citizens to return the favor with votes. Of course, once an immigrant becomes a citizen, the dependency cycle starts all over again with Progressive-supported policies like affirmative action.

CLASSICAL LIBERALS

The first thing to bear in mind when discussing immigration is to distinguish between legal and illegal immigration because Progressives don't want to make this distinction. Instead, they prefer to put all immigrants into one group in order to blur the distinctions between law-abiding immigrants and those who choose to enter and stay in America illegally.

Doing so obscures the fact that there are different types of immigrants with different methods for entering and enjoying our country. Since the law distinguishes between legal and illegal acts – and the people who commit them – you can too. Dividing the immigrant community into two easily identifiable groups has other advantages: it allows you to take the side of those following the legal process and become an advocate for reforms that will make their experience with our government as efficient as possible. More on that in a moment.

Focus on illegal immigration. It should be stopped for two reasons. First, because it rewards bad behavior in the form of free public education, in-state higher education tuition, and other social services provided at tax-payer expense to illegal immigrants. Second, because it tells people trying to immigrate legally that it's easier to violate the law and ask for amnesty later.

The best way to stop illegal immigration is to enforce the laws already on the books. That means scrupulously patrolling our borders and ports. It may sound obvious, but patrolling America's borders stops illegal entries into the country. It also drastically reduces the numbers of terrorists and drugs flowing into our nation.

Another key component of stopping illegal immigration is making mandatory employer compliance with the E-Verify system. The E-Verify system is a government database allowing employers to check the citizenship status of job applicants. If the applicant is not on the list, then the employer knows the applicant is in the country illegally. If the employer hires such an applicant the employer is subject to a heavy fine. Since the main attraction for illegal immigration is a comparatively rich source of jobs in America, one of the best ways to reduce the flow of illegal immigrant labor is to penalize employers from hiring them. The less jobs available means the less illegal aliens.

Back to our friends; the legal immigrants. It is important to point out the need to reform the current immigration system. There are two key changes that would have a dramatically positive effect. First, the quota system that determines how many foreign citizens from a particular country can immigrate in a given year should be changed to favor countries with cultures most similar to ours. By contrast, we should reduce the spots available for immigrants coming from countries that are not friendly to the United States, or whose culture is substantially different from ours.

The second reform should be to reduce the wait time for immigrants pursuing entry into the country legally. The current process for applying and being approved takes years of patiently navigating federal government bureaucracies for no real purpose other than an infatuation with process over people. In order to reduce wait times the procedure for screening immigrant applicants should be streamlined to make the process as direct and time efficient as possible. If more people from similar and friendly countries are allowed to immigrate, the security screening process will be that much easier to conduct.

It is not racist, bigoted, or inconsistent to argue for immigration laws to be enforced and reformed. While the color of one's skin should not give border screeners pause, the culture of an immigrant's home country should. We have always welcomed immigrants wanting to contribute to America. At the same time, we should be careful about admitting people from nations with governments or groups that would do us harm. Classical liberals are the friends of immigrants who see America as a City on a Hill, a Beacon of Freedom, and a Pearl of Great Price. We welcome those seeking political and economic freedom because in today's world, we need all the freedom-loving people we can get!

RESOURCES:

Know Thy Enemies

NATIONAL IMMIGRATION FORUM

http://www.immigrationforum.org/

REFORM IMMIGRATION FOR AMERICA

http://reformimmigrationforamerica.org/

Know Thy Friends

THE FEDERATION FOR AMERICAN IMMIGRATION REFORM (FAIR) (limit all immigration)

http://www.fairus.org/site/PageServer

CENTER FOR IMMIGRATION REFORM (limit all immigration)

http://www.cis.org/

HERITAGE FOUNDATION (limit illegal immigration)

http://www.heritage.org/research/immigration/; http://www.heritage.org/ Research/GovernmentReform/bg1807.cfm

AEI

http://www.aei.org/papers?page=1&rid=100018

Chapter 12

Global Warming and Cap & Trade: How to Tax America into Economic Collapse and Third World Status

What is cap and trade? Cap and trade is a solution in search of a problem. In order to understand what cap and trade is and why it is needed, you must first understand the reason it is proposed.

The climate is changing. In the 1970s it was getting too cold; in the 1990s, too hot. A decade into the new millennium there is no consensus on whether the globe is warming or cooling. In fact, some data suggest the world's temperature may have leveled off. One thing is for sure: there are an awful lot of measureable particles or compounds or emissions in the atmosphere. Some people think these are harmful to the planet. Many of these people want to reduce or eliminate them. One way to reduce the incentive to do something is to tax it. For example, if consuming energy creates more particles, compounds & emissions (PCE) in the atmosphere, then an energy tax would help to reduce its consumption that enable the PCE. But calling something a tax is unpopular. Conversely, supporting a "market" solution is very popular. That's why cap-and-trade schemes use the language of markets to sell themselves to politicians and the public.

PROGRESSIVES

Generally, Progressives support the idea of cap-and-trade (CAT). Basically, CAT is a government created "market" that starts when a "cap" on how much of a particular type of PCE can be released into the air. The amount of the allowable PCE between zero and the cap is given a numerical value. That value is then converted into a money-like currency called "credits". Those credits can then be used or sold (i.e. traded) among individuals and businesses that produce the capped PCE. In order to "spend" a credit, the owner of it produces the credit's amount of capped PCE. Once the PCE is released into the atmosphere, the credit is spent. Those with more credits than PCE production can sell their excess credits to those that want them.

Now, since the Government cap creates a scarcity (i.e. limited supply) of the PCE, the people who want but can't afford credits must find alternatives to the capped PCE because it's illegal to create more than the cap allows. In fact, many CAT supporters want the cap to increase over time to allow for fewer and fewer PCE, some as low as zero. Because of the scarcity, the price of credits will increase because the demand for them will increase while their supply stays the same or reduces. The rise in costs will price many people out of the PCE credit market. Some Progressives argue that the remaining free market will provide energy alternatives that are cheaper than buying PCE credits. Others argue for government subsidies to support alternative fuels if entrepreneurs won't – or can't – make a profit from them. Most Progressives, however, would rather see an overall reduction of energy consumption without creating a replacement. If that results in less wealth and/or less people, so be it. After all, these are the people who support population control; why not achieve it through economics?

Thus, the effect of a CAT system is to tax energy consumption that produces whatever is capped. Like all taxes, businesses won't pay it; consumers will. Think about the price of gas. Every time the Government tacks on a fuel, road, or environment tax, the energy companies pass the buck to you. They have to if they are going to make a profit. But why would Progressives want to tax energy? Look at whom the tax benefits: third world governments. Why? It is a way for the first world to pay off its "ecological debt."

"Ecological debt" or "climate reparations" are terms for redistributing first world wealth to the third world. Since the first world got rich during the Industrial Revolution and by exploiting third world human and natural resources, it's only right that it should now pay back – with interest – for its sins.

CLASSICAL LIBERALS

Remember the second fundamental law from the Core Principles? It said, "Do not encroach upon another person or their property." The same holds true for pollution. In yesteryear, when a company polluted the water, air, or ground and it affected another person's property, the injured person sued the company for damages. Moreover, if the pollution was especially dangerous, the injured party would sue for an injunction to stop the activity. Once enough lawsuits were successful, the company either cleaned up its operation or left town.

That system was pretty simple, and it served people well. The issues were straightforward and the outcomes depended on the skill of the attorneys, the clarity of the facts, and the reasonableness of a jury of citizens. The problem with CAT is that it rests on controversial theories about whether the substances to be capped are really pollutants, and thus injurious to human life. Since the science is not settled the fact are not clear. Furthermore, the reasonable jury is replaced with ideological bureaucrats whose job security is linked to finding new ways to regulate energy consumption. In fact, the only characteristic a CAT system shares with the previous practice of private litigation is the recourse to skillful lawyers.

CAT is not a free market. It is a government created market that arbitrarily determines the supply of PCE to advance a policy goal of reducing the existence of certain substances. The cost of doing so result in thousands of increased energy costs to American consumers, billions of lose revenue to businesses, and potentially trillions of transferred wealth to other countries. All of this, and the science on which CAT markets are based continues to be discredited either through Climate Gate or new data that conflicts with earlier projections.

RESOURCES:

Know Thy Enemies

ENVIRONMENTAL PROTECTION AGENCY (Page on Cap and Trade)

http://www.epa.gov/captrade/

SOUTHERN PEOPLE'S ECOLOGICAL DEBT CREDITORS ALLIANCE

http://www.ecologicaldebt.org/

ARTICLE: Socialists Demand Trillions in "Climate Debt"

http://www.aim.org/aim-column/socialists-demand-trillions-in-climate-debt/

Know Thy Friends

HERITAGE FOUNDATION

http://www.heritage.org/News/Cap-and-Trade-Global-Warming-Bill.cfm

ARTICLE: Beware of Cap and Trade Climate Bills (Heritage Foundation)

http://www.heritage.org/Research/Economy/wm1723.cfm

ARTICLE: Who Pays for Cap and Trade? (Wall Street Journal)

http://online.wsj.com/article/SB123655590609066021.html

Chapter 13

Energy Independence:
Destroying Home-Grown Nuclear, Gas, Oil & Clean Coal in Favor of Subsidizing Solar, Wind & Water Systems with Made-in-China Technology

PROGRESSIVES

We all know the world is ending because of man-made ~~global warming~~ climate change. In fact, as a species, we've been sowing the seeds of our own destruction since the Industrial Revolution. Our modern economy runs on some of the dirtiest sources of energy available: oil, coal, and natural gas. True, some people have made a lot of money from drilling and mining the earth to feed our insatiable appetite for consumer goods and energy, but the cost to the planet and its poorest humans is a deficit that must be repaid before it is too late. If we are serious about protecting the environment and the future health of our children, we need to act quickly to replace our dependency on oil, coal, and natural gas with clean technologies powered by solar, wind, and water systems.

The problems with oil, coal, and natural gas are that they are dirty and destructive to locate, harvest, process, and use. People who live in communities where drills, mines, and refineries are located are intimately aware of the dangers associated with these operations. Unsafe working conditions and rampant pollution make for much of the work of the Environmental Protection Agency. Moreover, the tax receipts from these companies are certainly outweighed by the aesthetic eyesore a factory creates.

Perhaps the biggest reason to pursue other forms of energy is the fact that we are dependent on other, non-friendly countries to supply our thirst for energy. That kind of dependency could put us in a terrible position of weakness if the wrong nation sought to link our energy with our submission. In a very real way, our energy policy is a crucial element of our national security policy. The more energy independent we are, the more discretion we will have to make our own decisions in foreign affairs.

For all these reasons we need to explore the benefits of solar, wind, and water-based energy technology. All of these are vastly superior in cleanliness and sustainability to oil, coal, and natural gas.

Now, we all know that businesses can't be expected to switch from using oil, coal, and natural gas to environmentally superior technologies using solar, wind, and water without a little prodding. After all, reducing profits for the sake of health and sustainability is not a hallmark of the private sector. That is why it is critically important to pass measures that reduce our dependency on these sources, so that the free market can develop cleaner, healthier technologies.

In order to speed up that process, the free market will need some help as well. Most government officials recognize this and support programs to fund conversions to a green economy. Part of that conversion would grant money to individuals and companies pursuing ways to reorient their manufacturing and service providing without using fossil fuels – or at least not as much.

Money will also be needed to propel more research attention towards finding ways to make clean and sustainable technologies more attractive and profitable. America's energy transformation won't be accomplished in a day, or maybe even a decade. But with a sustained focus on making our economy greener and cleaner, we will achieve our goals.

The earth's environment and our children's future are too important to sacrifice for the sake of preserving an energy company's profits. The time is now to begin the process of healing our planet and cleaning up our economy. It will take time to transition to cleaner, more sustainable energy technologies, but the longer we wait, the worse our situation will become. Some think that a citizen's greatest sacrifices are the ones she makes during a time of war. We think the greatest heroism is displayed when a country acknowledges its mistakes and sets about doing the hard work to make amends. Won't you join us?

CLASSICAL LIBERALS

The main problem with the Progressive pitch on energy reform is that they aren't asking people to join them in a voluntary association to develop an alternative economic model using "green" technology, the success of which would convince others to opt in. That would be a Classical Liberal approach. Instead, they cloak a dramatic increase in federal spending and regulation in their glossy appeal for popular support.

The Progressive critique of private business tells us something important about the energy market. If businesses can't be expected to switch to cleaner, greener energy, it's because "green" technology doesn't make financial sense. There are two reasons. First, solar, wind, and water-based energy cost too much for the average consumer to choose it over oil, coal, or natural gas. Second, even if those sources could be harvested for their maximum efficient use, there is not enough of any of them to meet the needs of our current economy. If Progressives were honest about the possibilities of sustainable energy, they would speak of a green-*er*, clean-*er* economy – one that supplements our use of oil, coal, and natural gas, not replaces it. The science doesn't support their claims, even with billions in government subsidies. Then again, what would Progressives be if not utopians?

Adopting the Progressive agenda for energy reform would lead to driving out profitable businesses, while skewing the domestic energy market towards taxpayer subsidized technologies. It would also replace the current supply system for our economy with sources that cannot hope to meet the same level of demand. The result would be more expensive energy for less people to consume. For a Classical Liberal, that formula doesn't add up. For a Progressive, though, it makes perfect sense. The reason lies in the true motivation for cleaner, greener technologies: Progressive guilt.

When Progressives talk about energy reform, their focus isn't on the economy – it's on the environment. They may claim to support their arguments with economic theories of supply and demand, but the truth is they think the demand is too high, so the supply should be diminished. Progressives think they and their fellow citizens consume too much. The solution, then, is to reduce consumption. That solar, wind, and water-based energy are cleaner than oil, coal, and natural gas because they produce less byproducts is a nice add-on. But it is by no means the motivation for the Progressive approach to energy policy.

Simply put, to Progressives, humans are locusts. In their view, we use entirely too much of our natural resources and the earth is getting tired of it. In fact, according to actor Danny Glover, the catastrophic January 2010 earthquake that rocked Haiti was a direct result of the world's failure to pass a comprehensive climate change treaty at the Copenhagen Convention. (If you don't remember it being reported, that's because Progressives in the mainstream media didn't think the statement was all that controversial.)

Since Progressives don't yet control the world, someone somewhere will fill the void left by Americans opting out of the traditional energy market. Just because Western governments have the fortitude to force their citizens to pay more for less, doesn't mean oil, coal, and natural gas producers like China, Russia, Iran, Saudi Arabia, and Venezuela think the same way.

An American opt out would further raise the economic and diplomatic prestige of these nations while marginalizing America's.

The real tragedy is that the United States don't have to be dictated to on energy supplies because the nation has vast stores of oil, coal, and natural gas just waiting to be extracted. From the Arctic National Wildlife Reserve (ANWR) to off-shore natural gas pools and shale oil in the interior West, America has plenty of energy; it just needs to be used. Don't let Progressives get away with projecting their guilt. We could all do a better job consuming energy, but we won't achieve much unless individuals are empowered to make a change, one decision at a time.

RESOURCES:

Know Thy Enemies

The Obama White House (Issues – Energy & the Environment)

http://www.whitehouse.gov/issues/energy-and-environment

THE SIERRA CLUB

http://www.sierraclub.org/

Know Thy Friends

THE HEARTLAND INSTITUTE (Environmental Policy Suite)

http://www.heartland.org/suites/environment/index.html

THE PROPERTY & ENVIRONMENT RESEARCH CENTER (PERC)

http://www.perc.org/

Chapter 14

Healthcare & Socialized Medicine:Welcome to Your National Health Service, Please Take a Number

PROGRESSIVES

The Progressive health care goal is for everyone to have the same kind for the same price. That's what European socialists were able to accomplish in most of their countries during the 20th century. Their American counterparts are feeling left out of the one-size-fits-all approach to medical coverage and treatment. The reasoning behind the desire is pretty simple: it's "fair" because it's "equal". Ultimately, Progressives want a universal, single-payer system, which means a tax-supported, government-run nationalized health care system. It's called single-payer because the Government collects all health care fees and pays for them through a single Government source. It's universal because it applies to everyone.

In Britain, that source is the National Health Service (NHS). It never seems to have enough money. Parties across Britain's political spectrum argue that the NHS needs more funding and more staff to reduce waiting times and improve treatment. In fact, reducing waiting times to see doctors and specialists is an evergreen issue in Britain. The reason lines are so long is because there aren't enough medical personnel and supplies to go around. That's one part of "rationing" care.

The other part is using government boards to determine who gets what treatment at what price and for how long. For example, if an elderly woman needs a hip replacement but her life expectancy is only five more years, the hearing board is very likely to deny her the hip replacement and provide pain killers instead. Why waste the time, effort, and supplies on a person who is statistically quite likely to be dead in a few years? Comfort has a cost that governments cannot afford.

Why is it like this? When the British Government became the sole provider of health care it capped salaries and took the profit motive out of the industry's calculus. That led to the reality that becoming a doctor no longer paid for the debt and hassles of medical school and residency. So now many of the best and brightest British minds aren't becoming doctors because they'll be paid a government wage. Far better to be a lawyer, a financier, or immigrant to America: at least then you'll be compensated in relation to the service you provide.

Progressives want the British NHS model because it treats equally all those British citizens not wealthy enough to leave the country for better medical treatment. The goal is a single payer system. The methods for getting there vary. Remember ObamaCare? When replacing the current American system with a single payer model became unpopular, Progressives retreated and proposed a "public option" that would compete with private insurance plans to lower prices. Unfortunately for private companies, the Government's public option wouldn't be priced in relation to its profitability. Thus, the public option could offer similar service for lower prices, regardless if it loses money. Eventually, private insurance companies would go out of business because they couldn't compete. Then, everyone would be forced into a single payer system.

When the public option became politically unfeasible, Progressives settled for an individual mandate. That requires everyone in the country to purchase health care coverage from a private insurance company. For those that cannot afford a plan, one will be paid for them by the Government. In the short run, the individual mandate is a boon (or giveaway) to private business. In the long run, it legitimizes the Federal Government's claim to be able to dictate individual health care decisions. Passing an individual mandate into law is not an obstacle to a single payer system. It only moves the finish line a little farther back than the public option. "Don't worry"; Progressives signal each other in the media. Single payer universal health care is coming. Be patient. The wait will just be a little while longer.

CLASSICAL LIBERALS

When it comes to receiving medical care, patience is seldom a virtue. Even the most minor injuries can lead to life-threatening conditions if left untreated. Thankfully, there is no requirement for people to wait in line while hurting, infected, or dying. There is a way to quicken the time it takes to get treated, by a good doctor, for an affordable price. As usual, it takes a market to free a people.

A free market approach to health care reform would maximize a health care consumer's choices. Information about doctor quality, medical outcomes, and the price of everything would be readily available. Medical histories would be digital, secure, and portable. Tax policy would not penalize people for putting their money in a Health Savings Account, or for being self-employed. Insurance policies would be purchasable and useable across state lines. If a doctor is licensed in one state she should be able to move her practice to another state and immediately start treating patients.

Most importantly, a free market in health care would bring transparency to an industry characterized by distortions in costs. Because most people receive their health insurance through their employer, the true price of their plan is hidden from them. First, they don't pay for the full cost of their plan because their employer contributes a hefty (and quickly forgotten) sum. Second, every visit to a doctor involves a flat, minimal payment called a co-pay. The other party (the "co") is the insurance company. After the employee finishes the appointment the doctor bills the insurance company for the full price of the visit.

Then the fun begins. Depending on a variety of factors, the amount paid by the insurance company is almost always lower than the original amount the doctor charged. Thereafter, a portion of the negotiated payment is billed to the employee. Since the employee has to pay only a fraction of the overall cost, he doesn't directly experience how much money he just spent. Moreover, the practice of negotiating insurance bill payments gives doctors an incentive to charge more than the actual cost plus profit because they know the insurance company will counter with a much lower payment offer. Thus, in order to make a profit, doctors must charge much more initially than they would otherwise.

This kind of price inflation is readily apparent to health care consumers who pay out of pocket. Because of the reduced transactions costs by cutting out the middle man (i.e. the insurance company), a doctor can charge his normal rate absent built-in inflation for negotiation. In this circumstance a consumer can ask how much a service costs before ordering it. If it is too much, the consumer can shop elsewhere. The key difference is that in this instance the consumer knows the true cost of the service he consumes. He can then make an intelligent decision about whether to purchase it or not. This is the freedom of choice a free market provides.

True, there will still be some treatments that are beyond the reach of most consumers' ability to pay. For these, one of two likely scenarios would come into play. One scenario would (re)create an insurance model of pooled risk to spread costs. However, if the employer were removed from the transaction consumers would be faced with more of the costs. If there were enough people needing a treatment that was too expensive, eventually the second scenario would arrive: an entrepreneur would figure out how to deliver the treatment cheaper. That's the scenario replayed in thousands of similar situations from I-Pods to prescription drugs. There is no reason to think high value medical treatments would be any different.

The best part about reforming our current health care system into a free market model is that it empowers individuals to choose from whom and for what price they will purchase health care. A universal, single-payer system does not – cannot – provide this kind of freedom. Like all other Progressive ideas, government-run health care is about empowering an elite at the expense of everyone else. Americans shouldn't pay the bill to enrich someone else's hubris.

RESOURCES:

Know Thy Enemies

CENTER FOR AMERICAN PROGRESS

http://www.americanprogress.org/issues/domestic/healthcare/

Know Thy Friends

CATO INSTITUTE

http://healthcare.cato.org/free-market-approach-health-care-reform

Chapter 15

The Second Amendment: The Citizen's Right to Own a Gun Protects the Entire Bill of Rights

BACKGROUND

In modern America most people interested in owning and using a gun must seek out opportunities to do so because many Americans do not live in an environment where guns are a normal part of everyday life. To be sure, some Americans are quite familiar with how to operate and maintain a gun. However, those living in urban and suburban settings are much less likely to appreciate the attraction and respect guns inspire. Conversely, many people are more likely to associate guns with video games and fictional violence than with conventional recreational pursuits like target practice or hunting. That kind of unfamiliarity has left many people open to disinformation about guns spread by Progressives.

PROGRESSIVES

Progressive arguments for "gun control" follow this pattern.

Guns are dangerous because people can use them to harm or kill others. In order to avoid anyone being harmed or killed by guns, private citizens should be banned from owning them. Instead, government agents should be the only people with guns because they can be trusted to use them properly.

Progressives argue that yearly gun-related deaths and horrific mass shootings like at Columbine or Virginia Tech support such a prohibition. After all, if guns weren't available to private citizens then none of these tragic events would have occurred.

But if private citizens can't be banned from owning guns, then there should be restrictions on who can own guns to keep them from winding up in the hands of people who will use them to hurt or kill others. For example, criminals and convicted felons should not be allowed to own guns because they have already shown a willingness to break the law. Committing a crime with a gun could lead to the injury or death of another person. Thus, there should be a waiting period between the time you purchase a gun and the time you receive it. In the interim, your background is checked to make sure you are not a criminal or convicted felon. If not, you get your gun.

However, before you receive it you must first get a license to own a gun. A license certifies that you meet the requirements to own a gun. You then must register your gun with the Government because it likes to know who has guns, how many, and what type(s). If you want to carry a concealed gun in one of the states that allows it, you will have to go through additional training and paperwork to get a permit to do so. When you complete all these steps, then you are allowed to possess your gun.

And if ownership restrictions don't eliminate the use of guns to hurt or kill others, then there should be restrictions on how guns are made and stored. Guns stored in homes should not only be kept in a gun safe, they should be equipped with trigger locks and/or disassembled to prevent an accidental firing.

It should be obvious at this point that Progressives really don't want private citizens to own guns because gun ownership scares them. A lot. In fact, most Progressives supporting "gun control" laws think that there must be something wrong with people who like to own, shoot, and hunt with guns. Guns are dangerous, didn't you know? And gun owners might get angry if non-owners try to regulate the former's use and enjoyment of guns. In fact, Progressives don't like the idea of millions of private citizens owning guns because it eliminates the Government's monopoly on the use of force; and the power to force opinions and practices on others is what Progressives are all about.

CLASSICAL LIBERALS

All gun-related human deaths are a tragedy. But guns don't hurt or kill people. People hurt and kill people. Guns are just some of the instruments some people use. Many times an injury or death resulting from a gun isn't a crime; it's an act of self-defense. Guns are dangerous, but they are also a deterrent. Widespread ownership of guns puts individuals – and the Government – on notice that a violent provocation stands a good chance of being met with a violent response.

America's Founding Fathers understood this aspect of gun ownership. In fact, they enshrined it in the Second Amendment to the Bill of Rights: "A well regulated militia, being necessary to the security of a free state, the right of the people keep and bear arms, shall not be infringed." Recently, the United States Supreme Court interpreted this to mean that the Second Amendment recognizes and protects Americans' pre-existing right to self-defense. That means the even before the Constitution became law, Americans had – and have – the right to keep and bear arms, and it shall not be infringed.

Of course, gun owners' rights are infringed by the kind of "gun control" laws promoted by Progressives. The problems begin with requiring gun owners to get licenses and register their guns. Granting a license implies that its giver has discretion to revoke it in the future. If the license is from the Government, and the right to possess a gun for self-defense predates the Constitution that created the Government, how can the Government restrict an American's right to own a gun for self-defense?

Even more problematic are gun registration laws. The idea behind gun registration laws is to alert the Government who has guns, how many, and what type(s). However, that information can easily be used to identify and confiscate guns from people the Government doesn't like. The transformation of registration lists into confiscation lists can be found in examples of Nazi Germany's treatment of Jewish gun owners, Soviet Russia's policy towards disfavored groups, and replicated by totalitarian regimes in Southeast Asia and Africa. If our Government were ever to slip towards an autocracy, one of the first steps would be rounding up the guns in order to eliminate the possibility of an armed opposition.

But before we get there, Progressives will try to make gun ownership so onerous that many people will forego their right to own a gun. One of the ways to do this is by requiring all guns kept at home to have a trigger lock. Supposedly, the lock makes the gun safer because it disables the trigger from being pulled to fire the gun. However, trigger locks violate one of the basic rules of gun safety: don't touch the trigger unless you are ready to fire. But in order to install or remove the trigger lock you must touch the trigger. In addition, locks can easily be defeated or become defective so that a locked trigger may actually be ready to fire. Apart from creating a false sense of safety when defective, when working trigger locks can also delay the owner's ability to use the gun for self-defense. That can hardly be what the Founders intended.

Indeed, it has been said that the Second Amendment protects all the others in the Bill of Rights, as well as those contained in the Constitution. This means that the Second Amendment recognizes a right of armed self-defense against not only other private citizens, but against the Government as well. Remember, the Founding Fathers who drafted and passed the Second Amendment had just fought a war against a government that sought to take their weapons in order to subdue them. In fact, the battles at Lexington and Concord erupted over the British army's attempt to confiscate the colonists' cache of muskets and cannon.

In 1996, the United Kingdom banned handguns when a deranged Scottish loner who had a long run-in with the law killed a number of grade school students and their teacher. It was the excuse that the government had been waiting for. The result? Illegal use of guns has exploded in the city centers as handguns for gang use become desirable to smuggle into Britain from Africa and Central America. For the ordinary street thug, the weapon of choice has become the knife. Fatal stabbings and disfigurement by knife wounds has exploded in crime statistics. Now the push is on to ban kitchen knives throughout the country. The long-standing but sadly unwritten British Bill of Rights had recognized the right of citizens to own guns. But this right, issued by the monarch, could be and ultimately was retracted by the Crown (the government). The "right" to bear arms turned out in the end to be just a "privilege" subject to the whim of the ruler in power.

As in Australia, which also disarmed its honest citizens with gun controls in the 90's, the number of thugs using guns to commit crimes has gone up, not down. In the US, armed robberies occur during the day when the homeowner (armed with his own defensive gun) is not likely to be at home to stop the crime. In the UK armed robbery now occurs at night - to be sure that the unarmed homeowner and family are there - so as to maximize the take. One thug holds the wife hostage while the husband is driven under gunpoint to his bank's ATM machine, where the other thug drains their bank accounts.

Like all issues, gun rights boils down to a battle between the Progressive desire for power versus the Classical Liberal's pursuit of freedom. Progressives fear their neighbors who would dare possess a gun because at bottom it represents a challenge to the Government's power. Classical Liberals, on the other hand, have no such fear because they realize that in America, the Government should be mindful of the people. Classical Liberals trust the people and fear the Government. Progressives fear the people and trust the Government (as long as they are in power).

RESOURCES:

Know Thy Enemies

BRADY CAMPAIGN TO PREVENT GUN VIOLENCE

http://www.bradycampaign.org/

THIRD WAY (FORMERLY AMERICANS FOR GUN SAFETY)

http://thirdway.org/

AMERICAN HUNTERS AND SHOOTERS ASSOCIATION

http://www.huntersandshooters.com/

COALITION TO STOP GUN VIOLENCE

http://www.csgv.org/

MAYORS AGAINST ILLEGAL GUNS

http://www.mayorsagainstillegalguns.org/html/home/home.shtml

Know Thy Friends

NATIONAL RIFLE ASSOCIATION

www.nranews.com/

NATIONAL ASSOCIATION FOR GUN RIGHTS

http://www.nationalgunrights.org/

ARTICLE: Trigger Locks are Dangerous

http://www.ralphdsherman.com/Press%20archive/98-09-12%20Hart-ford%20Courant.htm

ARTICLE: Trigger Locks Kill

http://www.wnd.com/news/article.asp?ARTICLE_ID=47462

ARTICLE: Federal trigger lock mandate

http://www.thefreelibrary.com/Federal+trigger-lock+mandate-a0150695784

PART III: THE BASICS

"No man's life, liberty, or property is safe while the legislature is in session."
-Mark Twain

You've read the core principles, and you're familiar with the current issues. Now, you know what needs to be done to re-found America. We need politicians and laws that respect the Two Fundamental Laws of Life, and protect our four types of property. We need educated citizens who demand allegiance to the Constitution from government officials, not just to the government itself. That is why we propose that along with your candidate questionnaires and scorecards, you ask any candidate seeking your support to take The Patriot's Pledge:

> "I pledge allegiance to the Constitution of the United States of America; to preserve, protect and defend against all enemies, foreign and domestic. I pledge that I will honor and bear true faith to the Constitution; that I take this obligation freely; and that I will well and faithfully discharge my duties of citizenship; so help me God."

If you are a member of a 9/12 group, or attend Tea Party meetings, suggest that The Patriot's Pledge be incorporated into your activities. It is an excellent way to focus attention on the document that distinguishes as Americans. Taking the pledge also helps to reinforce the first of four strategies for *Refound America* Patriots: Educate; Activate; Organize; Publicize.

First, we must educate ourselves and others. Next, we activate our families, friends, and neighbors into groups promoting faithful adherence to our Constitution. Then, we organize around a few key objectives targeted to increase freedom by supporting candidates, ballot initiatives, or institutions that honor our Constitution. Finally, we publicize our support through websites, blogs, political action committees, and media-friendly events.

You can make a difference. We will show you how.

Chapter 1 introduces the American public's number one enemy: Progressives. These are the people who created the Federal Reserve System that devalues our money, and passed a constitutional amendment to abolish the sovereign states' control over federal power. They followed that with another amendment creating a national prohibition of alcohol. Progressives want one thing: centralized control over your decisions. Thanks to Saul Alinsky and his *Rules for Radicals*, they have a process for achieving their goal. Ironically, all 13 rules can be used against Progressives. Game on!

Chapter 2 helps you find like-minded Patriots in your community through the power of social networking sites. Other freedom-loving citizens are just a few clicks away, and many are closer to your home than you might think. The popularity of Glenn Beck and his 9/12 Project are generating an explosion of grassroots activity online that you can – and should – tap into.

Chapter 3 explains how to reach out to friendly groups in your community. When building a movement for liberty, remember the importance of coalitions. While it would be great to get everyone involved with your group, there will be many people who are already committed to other organizations that share your mission. Go to them. Highlight the common bond that unites a liberty-loving Constitutionalist with Boy Scout troop leaders, American Legion members, and the local chapter of the National Rifle Association.

Chapter 4 takes your interest in activism and gives you quick keys to starting a group. Draft a mission statement, create an email address, and start collecting names. Planning and running meetings aren't hard skills to learn, but they do take forethought. After reading this chapter, you'll be ready to start leading immediately.

Chapter 5 tells you how to make it all happen. Like Saul Alinsky says in rule number six, "A good tactic is one your people enjoy." Activism should be fun. From senior citizen "die-ins" to hosting an "open-carry" party at Starbucks, we will give you the ideas to keep your fellow Patriots interested and entertained.

Chapter 6 gives you the scoop on capturing the media and your neighbor's attention. The key to communicating a clear, consistent message is to be clear and consistent. No joke. There's a reason people use talking points. They work. When you call a radio station or get interviewed by a local news station, you want to make sure you know your facts and your statements cold. That way you can stay on message no matter what the host or reporter says. Remember: your audience isn't the person with the microphone – it is the person listening on the other side of the radio or television.

Chapter 7 analyzes the genius of David Horowitz by applying his six simple principles for winning the war of ideas against Progressives *this year*. Horowitz was raised by Communists and followed its creeds until he realized how horribly wrong they are. Now, he devotes his energies to uncovering the insidious connections between business elites, political Progressives, and jihadist terrorists. He is on the front lines of the political and philosophical battle fields, and he has much to teach us.

Chapter 1

Progressives: What Every Patriot Should Know About Their History and Tactics

We are in a battle for personal freedom and the rule of law under The Constitution. We are fighting against a tribe of corrupt power-mad narcissists who want to tell you how to live your lives, raise your children, and run your businesses.

We call these people "Progressives", a benign-sounding word which masks the horrors of the 20th century that they brought upon us.

Make no mistake, true Progressives are radicals. Their hero is the now deceased radical Marxist community organizer and writer Saul Alinsky; a man who dedicated his book Rules for Radicals to Lucifer: "the first radical known to man who rebelled against the establishment and did it so effectively that he at least won his own kingdom". Hell!

When the average person is exposed to the truth about who the Progressives are and what they stand for, he is usually left in shock. They are not Democrats. They are not Republicans, although they have taken over rump groups in each party.

So, one of the strategies of the Progressives is to hide their true nature behind a sweet-looking mask. They've done this by systematically lying for decades about their not-so-secret past.

They've also systematically wiped out the teaching of American history and civics from our classrooms, and have forced textbooks to be adopted which compare George Washington to Chairman Mao as equal freedom-loving founders of their nations. The difference, of course, is that one of these people systematically murdered over 100 million people and the other established a society in which the rights of the citizen come above the wants of the government. Many children are confused today about who is who.

Although the Progressive movement can trace its history to the English Fabian Society, a group of Socialists active in the late 19th century, modern Progressives began with Teddy Roosevelt's Bull Moose Party of 1912 and his motto "speak softly, but carry a big stick". Rejecting social Darwinism, the early Progressives were driven to change the US Constitution to make society more "just". Fundamental rights such as the citizen's right to vote were admirably extended to women with the 19th Amendment ratified by the states on August 20, 1920. Then the Progressives nois-ily and unjustly took credit in the new progressive-dominated newspapers.

Big government, "the big stick" was also used to force through the previously unconstitutional federal income tax with the 16th Amendment ratified on February 3, 1913. Washington's revenues promptly jumped 1000% from $675 million in 1910 to $6.7 billion in 1920! With vast money comes vast power.

Contemporaneously, Congress passed the Federal Reserve Act on December 23, 1913, creating the national fractional banking system, al-lowing $10 to be lent for every real $1 held in the bank vaults. The inten-tional debasement of the dollar had begun.

Also in 1913, the 17th Amendment abolished the states' elected gov-ernments' link to their senators, with their election now made by direct vote instead. This strategy flipped upside down the Constitution - as it had originally and intentionally been designed by the founding fathers. This sad Amendment was ratified by the states on April 8, 1913.

By doing so, the states gave up their veto control over the future fed-eral behemoth - which they had originally given birth to. They had ef-fectively become appendages, mere vassal states of the all-powerful center. Bottom-up power which had emanated from the people and their state-houses was replaced with top-down control by Washington. The Senate, long the representative and protector of the individual sovereign states, became another federal government power center. The die had been cast.

Flushed with success, the Progressives then forced through the dis-aster of Prohibition, making it illegal for anyone in the United States to be able to drink alcohol "for the good of the people" who were too ignorant to know what was good for them. The 18th Amendment was ratified on January 16, 1919. During the 13 years it took for Article 21 to repeal this Progressive disaster on December 5, 1933, the Mafia had become fully en-trenched - offering the American people a market for what their govern-ment said they couldn't have legally.

So by their actions, the Progressives created organized crime as we know it today.

Did they do this foolishly with no understanding of human nature or the natural law of "for every action there's a reaction"? Or did they do it intentionally, knowing that creating the opportunity for the Mob to exist would then give the Progressives the opportunity to establish a national government police force: the FBI? The FBI would quickly turn into a political weapon used against it's enemies in Washington by director-for-life J. Edgar Hoover. So were the Progressives merely stupid - or evil?

By 1924, the Progressive movement had been taken over by Senator Robert M. La Follette of Wisconsin and his Conference for Progressive Political Action (CPPA). The Socialists, the Farmer-Labor Party, and a variety of labor unions co-opted the CPPA, which expanded the movement into the Progressive Party.

The Progressives stood for taking over the Judiciary that was overturning the unconstitutional laws being passed by Progressives in Congress. They argued for "agricultural reform" to eliminate over-productivity (yes, you read that right) by paying farmers not to grow food. They argued for "tax reform" to penalize people who worked harder to make more money by taking away a higher percentage of their income - not just a greater amount - thus giving birth to the "progressive" income tax.

And they called for government ownership of the nation's railroads, coal, oil and ore fields, timber forests, and hydroelectric dams. They got what they wanted.

Then came Franklin D. Roosevelt, Jr., and his "New Deal" socialism. It was FDR who seized the gold coins in Americans' pockets. It was Roosevelt who broke the back of the Supreme Court by threatening to expand its numbers to 17, and add 8 of his cronies to the bench. Now in control, it was FDR who forced the re-interpretation of the "commerce clause" of the Constitution to strip away the rights of the sovereign states and give the federal government massive new powers not intended by the founding fathers.

And it was Roosevelt who was elected four times to the Presidency. He died in office. After his death, in gratitude to his service, the American people quickly passed the 22nd Amendment to prevent a dictator-for-life to ever be elected again. During World War II, FDR was the Progressive president who unconstitutionally locked up American citizens in prison camps. Americans whose names were hyphenated: Japanese-Americans, German-Americans and Italian-Americans. Just like the Communists in the USSR and the Nazi's in Germany.

For years, the Progressives and Marxists have been agitating and organizing to overthrow America and the US Constitution.

The aging hippies of the 1960's, now in their sixties, have become university professors, journalists, union organizers and community activists. They have infiltrated the most sacred parts of our society, our schools, teaching our children what to think rather than how to think. They have taken over the so-called main stream media and the White House press corps, where from 80% to 90% vote Democrat. They have taken over Wall Street, where most of the fat-cats are registered Democrats and heavily support the Progressives.

Progressives have brainwashed our children into believing false-hoods like *An Inconvenient Truth*, the supposed documentary promoted by Al Gore for his own financial benefit as the chief beneficiary of his London-based "Cap and Trade" business, Generation Investment Management LLP, run with his partner David Blood, the former Goldman Sachs CEO.

And the Progressives have faithfully followed the teachings and strategy of Saul Alinsky. They are statists, in love with the idea of the big-brother and big-nanny state, who will lovingly take care of everyone, once they, the smarter citizens, are in charge. But God help you if you disagree with their vision of "Utopia".

Alinsky's progressive handbook, *Rules for Radicals*, shows step-by-step how a tiny percentage of the society can take over the system from within and bring it crashing down. It's true that the squeakiest wheel gets greased first. And Progressives whine at the drop of a hat.

Pretending to be ever so concerned for their fellow citizen, they prey on the innocent and gullible by promising to take care of them - on the condition that the Progressives are given the power to rule - absolute power.

Regular rank-and-file Progressives are often narcissistic. World-class Progressive leaders are usually sociopaths. In Transactional Analysis terms (*I'm OK, You're OK*), the progressive personality takes the position: "I'm OK, You're Not OK". He's right - and you don't really exist. Thus, the Progressive does not accept criticism easily, but rather seeks to crush all opposition either physically or with dismissive language like "global warming is settled science", or "home schooling creates bigots". Progressives lie, cheat and steal to achieve these ends, because, as Marx said: "the means justify the ends", no matter how many people are harmed or killed along the way. "You have to break a few eggs to make an omelet". Hmmm, hmmm, hmmm, tasty!

The Progressives under the guise of Marxism murdered several hundred million people in the 20th century. They lust for power. Wherever they come to power: Russia, China, Cambodia, Zimbabwe, Cuba, North Korea, East Germany, the result has been the same. One-party rule, elimination of the free press, no freedom of worship, secret police, suffering, torture, "re-education camps", massive cronyism & corruption, starvation & death are their hallmarks.

The irony is that Saul Alinsky's tactics to take over power can be used for good as well as evil.

Make no mistake. Alinsky was a profoundly amoral person. His 3 rules on the ethics of means and ends taught that 1) the more people are involved with an issue the less they will care about what means they use to win, 2) judgment about what's moral or immoral is determined by who's in control, and 3) "in war, the end justifies almost any means".

The idea of natural law, of God-given rights meant nothing to Alinsky. Alinsky enjoyed revolution for revolution's sake. He lusted after change - for change's sake alone. This lust for the raw power to destroy can be seen in the little boy who enjoys smashing his grandfather's gold watch but is too ignorant to know how to build a new one.

The 13 Rules for Radicals

Alinsky's developed a magic formula, his 13 rules for revolution, to effect change. 12 years after his death, one of his budding young followers became a teacher of his methods to engage progressive community activists. His name was Barack Obama. You, the patriot activist, can also use Alinsky's own methods to turn them against the Progressives - and to take back America, morally.

According to Alinsky, the principal job of an organizer is to bait the opponent into reacting. "The enemy properly goaded and guided in his reaction will be your major strength." Here are his 13 rules:

1. Power is not only what you have but what the enemy thinks you have.

It's like playing poker. Successful negotiators know that power can be real or imaginary. And power to motivate people usually comes from fear or greed. Are there 10 million tea party members - or 100 million? When you talk with the media, are you representing the dozen friends standing next to you - or the 10,000 local activists waiting around the corner?

2. Never go outside the experience of your people.

Make sure that you lead your team in ways that they understand and can support. Know their strengths, but also their limitations. Asking a busy mother to take part in a day-long demonstration might not work; asking her to blog on the Internet in her fleeting spare time would.

3. Whenever possible, go outside the experience of the enemy.

Try to cause confusion, fear and retreat. General Patton made far-flung sweeps with his American Third Armored Division deep into German territory during World

War II. Infiltrate the Progressive's meetings and then show up with protestors at the next big public event.

4. Make the enemy live up to their own book of rules.

Although a Progressive is often morally confused, they pretend to uphold moral values - especially when they promote their ideas in the media. If they say that human life is sacred to them and they are against euthanasia or capital punishment, then challenge them about abortion. If they say they support women's rights, then make them take a position on enforced wearing of hijabs and burqas by Muslim religious police. Point out the inconsistencies and hypocrisy in their own relativistic beliefs.

5. Ridicule is man's most potent weapon.

Progressives have notorious thin skins. In the extreme, progressive personalities have been known to resort to violence and even foam at the mouth with anger. They can't laugh at themselves. Thus a good strategy is to ridicule and make fun of them. Cartoons, clever bumper stickers and witty signs can work wonders.

6. A good tactic is one that your people enjoy.

You should always have fun in what you do. The Constitution guarantees our right to "life, liberty, and the pursuit of happiness". Take advantage of it. You're a wise and loving parent and the Progressive is a little brat caught up in his own ego. Remind him of it. And never forget to laugh at yourself too.

7. A tactic that drags on too long becomes a drag.

Keep changing the mix. Be creative. Turn on your imagination. Rotate strategies, events, tactics. It's more fun - and it throws off the opposition.

8. Keep the pressure on.

Do something. Then do another thing. Then do a third thing. Overwhelm the Progressives with too many things so they can't respond to everything at once. Not all of them are unemployed or students. Many even have jobs too - in schools, the media and big bureaucracies. They might even be busy doing other things too.

9. The threat is usually more terrifying than the thing itself.

Like the Wizard of Oz, most things operate with a certain amount of bluff, smoke and mirrors. Progressives get downright cocky and arrogant when they think that they are in the majority. Like the bully, they will often turn tail and run away to hide when they see that the overwhelming number of patriots in the country are against them.

10. The major premise for tactics is the development of operations that will maintain a constant pressure upon the opposition.

Let's say you are going to take on a progressive blog (one of the strategies discussed later on). Write a reply comment refuting, reflecting and belittling the blog each and every day. That daily pressure forces the readers - and the original writer - to reflect just a bit on the fact that there's pushback to their flimsy ideas. And user humor, not insults.

11. If you push a negative long and hard and deep enough it will break through its own counterside.

Alinsky gives the example of India's Mahatma Gandhi's development of the idea of passive resistance. This tactic is usually unsettling to the other side which is impatient, and eager for change - and now.

12. The price of a successful attack is a constructive alternative.

Sometimes the other side might use a deflecting strategy; "you're right, now tell us what to do." Be prepared to answer constructively step-by-step.

13. Pick the target, freeze it, personalize it, and polarize it.

This is the most famous of the Alinsky dictates. When you argue, form an image of a person, not a thing or building. Then isolate that person and focus on how out-of-touch their beliefs really are from mainstream America. You are against Barack Hussein Obama and Nancy Pelosi and Harry Reid, not the White House or Congress or Democrats. You are for George Washington, Thomas Jefferson, Benjamin Franklin, not the founding fathers. Progressives continue to target George Bush as their evil enemy, and blame him - even though he's been out of office for over a year.

Some notable Statists to remember: Stalin, Mao, Pol Pot, Kim Jong-il, Castro, "Che" Guevara, Hitler. Murderers and bullies every one. Many Progressives hold one or more of these psychopaths up as their heroes. Good "Progressives" all. Associate them whenever possible with the modern-day Progressives in Washington. It's easy to do - and true.

Saul Alinsky's little book Rules for Radicals: A Pragmatic Primer for Realistic Radicals is available at most bookstores. But a far better book is David Horowitz' brilliant counter-strategy analysis: Barack Obama's Rules for Revolution, the Alinsky Model. You can order a copy for $5.95 from www.horowitzfreedomcenter.org, or download your own free PDF copy (56 pages) from our special website: www.RefoundingAmericaBook.com by using the unique code found on the last page of this book.

In the following four chapters, we provide practical, hands-on strategies and techniques to turn your patriotic activism loose to take back America.

Chapter 2

How to Connect Up with Other Patriots

You are not alone! There are literally tens of millions of other patriots throughout America. There are tens of thousands of like-minded citizens nearby. Even in California.

How to find them? How can you link up with other freedom-loving individuals and families to take back America together? Easy.

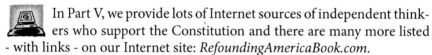 In Part V, we provide lots of Internet sources of independent thinkers who support the Constitution and there are many more listed - with links - on our Internet site: *RefoundingAmericaBook.com*.

First place to visit: *RefoundingAmericaBook.com*. Use the special code found on the last page of this book, and create your own free account. This will give you access to gobs of links, sites, contacts, groups, events, and information on how to fight for freedom in your own community and nationwide.

Next, go to *GlennBeck.com* to keep up with his latest announcements and clips from his important radio & TV shows. Be sure to check out Glenn's Twitter account at *twitter.com/glennbeck*. Over 175,000 people are plugged in.

Also be sure to visit his Facebook account at *facebook.com/glennbeck*. Over 550,000 people are connected here. Then, click over to Glenn's *the912project.com* and follow the links to find lots of other groups and sites to check out. If you haven't done so yet, sign up for free accounts with each of these networking sites.

Now, check out *www.meetup.com*. This is one of the goldmines of social networking! Create your own free account and log in. Then use the search engine to find 912, Tea Party, We the People and other patriot activist groups near you. Start with: "Glenn Beck 912 We Surround Them". You will find 39,736 groups. Enter just "912 Project" and you'll find another 2,780 Meetup Groups. There are 5,798 "Tea Party" groups, and thousands of more groups of Tea Party Patriots nationwide. Many of these will have duplicate entries but you get the picture!

So, let's check out the Meetup Groups which get together in, say, San Antonio, Texas. Searching under "9/12 Project" for zip code 73301, we find that there are 11 groups within a 25 mile radius which might match up. The second group is a good place to start. It's called the Central Texas 9-12 Project, and has over 400 members.

The group's organizer lives about 6 miles away on the other side of town. Their goals are to seek "the restoration of freedom and liberty as originally provided for in the principles of limited government set forth by 'We the People' in the US Constitution". They meet up every few weeks at a local restaurant, and post a calendar of other 9/12 groups which have weekly meetings throughout Austin.

They hold seminars, show films, have discussion groups, and plan and do activist projects and outreach programs, demonstrations and media events locally. Sounds like a good group to check out.

Ning.com is another social networking site with lots of Patriot activist group activity. Like Meetup, after creating your own free account, you can sign on to start a new group or find other similar groups nationwide.

Searching under the Politics category, you'll soon come upon multiple Ning groups with members who you can connect with. Like Meetup, Ning groups can arrange to physically meet up locally, but this social networking service is more Internet oriented. At *rebuildtheparty.ning.com*, over 4500 members get together on the Internet to plan to retool the Republican Party into a Patriot-activated "we the People" organization. Their online calendar is full of meetings being held every week throughout the country. And you're invited.

Facebook.com has similar Patriot groups which can be found using their search function. Entering 912, for example, provides 5100 groups with 912 in their name, most of which are associated with the national Glenn Beck 9/12 movement.

Ron Paul's *CampaignForLiberty.com* is an activist organization creating local groups and coordinators for conservative and libertarian supporters of like-minded candidates and issues. The site has lots of videos, free downloads of complete books on PDF's, forums, and materials for Patriot activists. Particularly good resources on economics, sound money, libertarian foreign policy, the Constitution, civil liberties, and education freedom.

The *Campaign For Liberty* has over 100,000 active members nationwide. They are recruiting, training and equipping 180,000 leaders for each precinct in the United States to advance the cause of freedom on a permanent basis from now on. Ron Paul has for many years been a lone voice speaking up in Congress for the Constitution and limited government.

Nicknamed "Dr. No" (he was a baby doctor who has delivered over 3,000 babies into the world) by his colleagues, Ron Paul votes against any bill that has no basis within the Constitution. Unfortunately, this means that he votes "no" 90% of the time! Now, he has established a national grassroots organization to invite join him in he battle. We invite you to join *Campaign For Liberty*.

The Heritage Foundation has nearly a million active members and friends who get their free myHeritage.org e-Newsletters on freedom and liberty. Heritage.org is loaded with how-to information for Patriot activists, starting on their home page with their Leadership for America 10 Transformational Initiatives. If there ever was an organization worth connecting up with, it's the Heritage Foundation and their Community Committees located throughout the US.

The Leadership Institute trains student and adult Patriot activist leaders in its nationwide training schools. It helps start patriotic groups on campuses nationwide through its campusreform.org program. If you have college-age children or friends, have them join their local campus group. You can also give them some local support - and it's a great way to tap into the energy (and time) of the college-age generation. For upcoming training programs, television workshops, local activities and resources, go to LeadershipInstitute.org immediately.

In the next Chapter, we provide another 12 groups which have local chapters of people that you can get to know as friends. You are not alone.

Chapter 3

How to Reach Out to Friendly Groups

There are many local groups throughout the United States which share similar values and support the Constitution and our personal liberties as protected by the Bill of Rights. These groups have local meeting halls and buildings where their members get together. They are part of their national organizations who usually have active lobbying organizations in Washington and the 50 state capitols.

Contact as many of these local groups as you can. Go to their national web site and locate a local chapter using their search-by-zipcode function. Optionally, give their national office a phone call. They often post their toll-free telephone numbers. Try the membership departments and the outreach coordinators. And while you're at it, have them mail you a package of materials about their organization, and what they're presently doing to support freedom and the Constitution.

Many of these organizations will also have meeting rooms that they can make available to you and your local Patriot group for free! In fact, holding your meetings in, say, the local American Legion hall will be well received. You can reach out to their members by inviting them to attend and by making presentations to their own membership at their next meeting.

Let's take a look at The American Legion. Most of the Legion's members are retired and not terribly active. Out of, perhaps 500 members, usually far fewer will regularly attend meetings. Strategy: invite them all to attend a special meeting where you can introduce your group. Show a DVD documentary or series of YouTube video clips followed by an open discussion of your activities and call for support and action. You will be pleasantly surprised by the positive response. In fact, based on first-hand experience, Legion members are just waiting for such an opportunity as fellow patriots to chip in and lend a hand.

And since most members of the American Legion are retired, they will have substantial time available to get on the telephone and work the internet as well as come out to take part in public demonstrations and events. They will also be fearless. After all, they've been to war and risked their lives to save America. They will be proud to do it again at home - if you only ask them.

So action item #1 is: call one or more of your local American Legion halls and speak to them about what your group is doing - and how you need their help!

Here are the top friendly local groups to reach out to:

1. The American Legion

The American Legion was chartered and incorporated by Congress in 1919 as a patriotic veterans organization devoted to mutual helpfulness. It is the nation's largest veterans service organization, committed to mentoring and sponsorship of youth programs in local communities, advocating patriotism and honor, promoting a strong national security, and continued devotion to fellow service members and veterans. The American Legion's first and foremost goal is "to uphold and defend the Constitution of the United States of America".

The American Legion has 2.5 million members, and 14,200 posts with over 8,000 local meeting Halls.

To locate your local American Legion Post, go to *Legion.org*.

2. The National Rifle Association

Dismayed by the lack of marksmanship shown by their troops, Union veterans Col. William C. Church and Gen. George Wingate formed the National Rifle Association in 1871. The primary goal of the association would be to "promote and encourage rifle shooting on a scientific basis". Since then, the NRA maintains active local offices and coordinates with gun clubs throughout the US.

While recognized today as a major political force and as America's foremost defender of Second Amendment rights, the NRA has, since its inception, been the premier firearms education organization in the world, with over 4.3 million members. It is also the defender of right-to-carry and concealed weapons permits being issued to law-abiding citizens.

Barely 15 years ago, only a few US states recognized their citizens' right to carry a concealed weapon for personal protection. Today, 40 states now recognize this right with the remaining holdouts being the historic socialist-oriented states: New York, California, Illinois, Michigan, etc. Since it has been said that the 2nd Amendment protects the other nine Amendments in the Bill of Rights, the NRA is certainly the foremost defender of personal freedoms in America.

During any given week, there will be perhaps dozens of activities, events, meetings and other opportunities to meet up with NRA members.

There are over 11,000 active local NRA groups.

To locate your local NRA group, go to *nraila.org* and click on 'Take Action'. Then select 'Get Involved Locally', and enter your zip code to locate your local Election Volunteer Coordinator and give him or her a call to find out what's going on locally.

Other NRA web sites with meeting information are: *NRA.org* and *FriendsOfNRA.org*.

Gun Owners of America (*GunOwners.org*), while not a local chapter organization, is also an active Washington lobby group with over 350,000 members nationwide. Ron Paul calls GOA "the only no-compromise gun lobby in Washington". A good source of information and support for issues-oriented Patriot activist groups.

3. Masons & Masonic Lodges

Freemasonry is one of the oldest fraternal organizations in the United States, and it claims many of the Founding Fathers – as well as other luminous business and political figures since then – as members. The organization is well-known for philanthropic activities like disaster relief and hospital visitations. It also provides a place for religiously-minded men to pursue high ethical standards while learning to be better husbands, fathers, and neighbors.

The Masonic Service Association of North America (*MSANA.com*) is a national organization that provides links to state-specific Grand Lodges – the point of contact for people looking for more information and locations for local lodges.

4. Boy Scouts of America

The year 2010 marks the centenary of the Boy Scouts of America (BSA). With over 4 million youth members in its ranks – and over 110 million Americans having participated in its programs over the years – BSA trains scouts to be responsible citizens, cheerful helpers, and self-reliant. Simply put, BSA helps mold its youthful members into people of strong character, and ardent patriots. Any parent who would want their child to receive formation from the Boy Scouts is a natural fit for our movement.

If you have a child in a local Boy Scout troop, take the opportunity to speak with other parents about the benefits of raising kids in such a patriotic, wholesome environment. It will provide a great segue into discussing the need for similar values in our political system. We need people of character in Washington, D.C., and our state capitols willing and able to argue for the dignity of the individual work ethic and the importance of local, civil society solutions to problems. People drawn to the spirit of BSA or GSUSA are natural partners in our push for a freer, more prosperous country. Finding your local scouting affiliate is as easy as visiting *Scouting.org*.

Unfortunately, many Girl Scout groups (GSUSA) seem to have lost their way. Some have been taken over by Progressives. So, if you have a teenage daughter, you'll need to be careful in checking out the values of the local troop. See: *GirlScouts.org*.

5. Home School Parents

The home schooling movement is one of the fastest-growing sectors of K-12 education. Nearly all of these parents have lost faith in the tax-supported public school system to adequately education – and in some cases, protect – their children. For many of these parents, private school is not a viable alternative. So, they do what Americans have always done when they are in need of a solution that no one else is providing: do it themselves.

At its core, the home schooling movement is a response to government's failure to provide a values-based, traditional education in a safe learning environment. In many ways, home school parents are the educator equivalent to the pioneering spirit that ventured out and settled the American frontier. It's an ethos that predates the founding of our country: if there isn't room for you or your ideas in the current system, set out to find and make your own. Parents who home school do the same thing when they elect to take the education of their children under their own direct care. While it's not a path followed by everyone, the trail these people blaze increases the educational options for all Americans. For that, we should all be grateful.

One of the defining characteristics of home school families is their deep sense of patriotism. In fact, a key topic of conversation is often how to instill fundamental American values like thrift, hard work, and love of country in children. These are patriot activists! They are not waiting for public education to fix itself – they are taking matters into their own hands, and producing better, more knowledgeable students than the public school system.

So, get to know these people. They are your neighbors, fellow church-goers, and co-workers. They know the importance of getting involved, and they will be eager to assist in your project to Refound America. And make sure to listen; we could all learn some things about perseverance, organization, and innovation from people who are rethinking – and remaking – K-12 education.

You can start by searching for your state's home school association website, and looking for local events where home school parents meet. Attend one of these and ask if they're interested in applying the lessons they've learned from enriching the home school movement to the political arena. Tell them we patriots must stick together in the fight against more government takeovers of our freedoms. If they don't already know about it, mention *HSLDA.org* – the Home School Legal Defense Association. It's a public interest law firm that defends the rights of home school families. With this you'll make a friend. Next, make an ally.

To find your State's local homeschool association and lots more information, see: *homeschooling.about.com/library/blassocusa.htm.* Also visit the incredible Robinson Curriculum at: *oism.org/s32p28.htm.* It's endorsed by Ron Paul, a friend of the family.

6. Veterans & VFW lodges

The Veterans of Foreign Wars of the United States boasts 2.2 million members in 8,100 posts around the world. Founded in 1899 to assist veterans of the war and insurrection in the Philippines, the VFW continues to help veterans from all of America's wars hence. It also lives its motto – "honoring the dead by helping the living" – by helping to establish the Veterans Administration, create the G.I. Bill, and improve VA hospitals.

As evidenced by their service to America, VFW members are patriots of the first order. They care deeply about their country, and are committed to helping preserve the values and traditions they fought to protect. Finding support among these fellow patriots is only a few clicks away. After visiting the *VFW.org*, look for the link that says "Find a VFW Post Website". (Bear in mind, not all posts have websites.) Then, look for the nearest post, and attend their next meeting. Many of the events are social gathering featuring food, dancing, and service-oriented activities. One of their future activities could be helping you Refound America!

VeteransNetwork.net/directory.php is another great resource for finding veterans groups, as is www1.va.gov/vso/index.cfm?template=view, a listing of veterans groups from the Veterans Administration website.

7. Places of Worship

Patriot activists are most likely to come from the ranks of people who – like Edmund Burke – cherish tradition and respect the value of religion. You may recall that many American pulpits thundered approval of the colonists' cause in the run-up to the Revolution of 1776. Americans are bred in the bone to love liberty and oppose tyranny. Even today, people of faith are at the forefront of the limited government movement arguing for a more robust role for civil society organizations like charities, churches, and synagogues.

The best place to start is at your own place of worship. If you don't attend one, or are looking for places to branch out, use the "Search Nearby" feature on Google Maps at *Maps.Google.com*. If you want to quickly narrow your search to a particular Christian denomination or set of denominations, *USAChurch.com* and *WorshipQuest.org* can each give you several listings depending on your search criteria.

If looking for possibly sympathetic synagogues, *USCJ.org* is a good place to start for finding Conservative Jewish synagogues, while *OU.org* is a good resource for finding Orthodox synagogues.

Additionally, Mormon Churches are very supportive of promoting traditional American values. They are a terrific resource for organizing and contributing to patriotic endeavors. To find the nearest Meetinghouse near you, go to *Maps.LDS.org*.

If Catholic, then check out your local Knights of Columbus chapter at *KofC.org*. The Order was founded over 125 years ago to give Catholic American men a place to grow spiritually through service to others. From parish pancake breakfasts to international disaster relief, Knights are committed to helping make the world a better place through high quality volunteerism. If you know a Knight, you know someone in love with his Church, his country, and his community.

8. Law Enforcement Rank-&-File Groups

Other than the military, there may not be a group of people who serve Americans more honorably than law enforcement officers. Each day, many of them risk their lives enforcing the law and providing order. It takes a special kind of person to physically oppose evil in our communities so that the rest of us can focus on expanding those efforts that promote human flourishing. In order for freedom to prosper, someone has to make sure that peace and stability are the norm. Those people are our policemen and women.

There are several good national websites that allow you to drill down into state and local levels to find the patriotic police groups nearest you! *Officer.com* lists law enforcement associations from across the country, as does *Google.com/Top/Society/Law/Law_Enforcement/Organizations*. Once you find your local police forces, do an internet search for their union and Political Action Committee contact information. The people that run these will be in the best position to tell you how to reach their members. Emphasize that you wish to present a speech thanking the officers for their continued service, and spelling out ways your group can partner with theirs. Appeal to members as citizens who love their country and are dedicated professionally to protecting it. Try to identify whether the group is supportive of gun rights for private citizens, and lower taxes. In short, find ways to turn your shared patriotism into a specific political issue. When you do, you will have a powerful ally.

9. Tax Revolt Groups

One of the most popular acronyms used in Tea Party rallies is Taxed Enough Already! It is a sentiment that echoes back to a frigid night in Boston Harbor where Sons of Liberty made the bay run sweet with His Majesty's high tax tea. It was a battle cry heard in the 1970s when grassroots activists like Howard Jarvis awakened California homeowners from their slumber to protest out-of-control property tax increases. The passage of Proposition 13 in 1978 set off a nationwide revolt against rapacious government taxes and spending. You can read all about it at *HJTA.org*.

The movement became so popular that an actor, union president and former Democrat was elected President of the United States. Ronald Reagan asked Grover Norquist to create a national organization dedicated solely to lowering taxes, and Americans for Tax Reform, *ATR.org*, was born. Now, there are several groups pursuing lower taxes, including the National Taxpayers Union, *NTU.org*. Each of these groups provide excellent educational resources for getting up to speed on the myriad of ways governments reach into your pocketbook. After you master the information, contact one of these and ask if you can start a local chapter. Start putting pressure on local politicians to consider spending cuts instead of tax hikes. Tell them that taking more money from people with less of it doesn't make sense. After all, we're Taxed Enough Already!

10. Small Business Groups

Small business is the engine of our economy. Big corporations may be more familiar, but small businesses are the innovators and the job creators. They are also the most sensitive to tax and regulatory policies because their profit margins are not as wide as larger companies. An increase in either area could be devastating to a small business's ability to compete and make a profit. They may be small in number of workers each business employs, but they know how to organize.

NSBA.biz is the website for the National Small Business Association which has an "affiliates" link that allows you to search for state level branches. Depending on the state website, you can then identify local small businesses that are motivated to lobby for less regulation and taxes. These people are our friends! And so are businesses affiliated with *Cose. org* – the Council of Smaller Enterprises.

11. Chambers of Commerce

Any business can belong to a chamber of commerce. The best place to start is *USChamber.com* because it is the largest, most influential organization on behalf of business interests. You can find a directory of local affiliated chambers at *USChamber.com/chambers/directory/default.* Other helpful websites are the United Hispanic Chamber of Commerce at *USHCC.com*, and the National Black Chamber of Commerce at *NationalBCC. org.* Hint: you can join your local chamber of commerce whether or not you own a small business.

More than any other business group, chambers of commerce are heavily active in communities across the country. These activities take the form of service projects, educational events, and political awareness campaigns. Politicians routinely make speeches to chamber groups, and many of them seek endorsements. Since chambers are primarily concerned with creating and maintaining a thriving business environment, their members will be receptive to your free market ideas.

This will be especially true in areas where businesses are heavily taxed. In fact, you may find that chamber members are angered by increasing regulations that make it difficult to do business – so much so that they will be eager to learn more about your ideas to campaign for more economic freedom. Like any regularly meeting organization, a chamber of commerce is always looking to fill speaker slots. Find the ones nearest you, and schedule a speech soon!

12. Amateur Radio Operators

If the world were to end tomorrow, you'll want access to three things: water, food, and an amateur radio operator. Operators are ordinary citizens with an abiding interest in communicating via radio waves. Many of these people are self-taught engineers capable of building powerful transmitters which can reach others thousands of miles away. That could come in handy in case our modern telecommunications system ever fails or is destroyed. Amateur radio operators (i.e. "ham" operators) were the communications service that allowed law enforcement and private citizens to coordinate their search and rescue teams after the September 11th bombing, Hurricane Katrina, and countless other disasters.

Like most of the groups on this list, amateur radio operators are private citizens just like you who educate themselves about something to the point of becoming an expert. They then use their expertise to have fun and help others. These are our kind of people! *ARRL.org*, and *QSL.net/races* are two great places to find local "Ham" operators in your area.

There are lots of active local groups which often meet up to practice voluntary community emergency coordination, like RACES (Radio Amateur Civil Emergency Service). See: *USRaces.org*. Arrange to speak to your local Ham groups on our 1st Amendment Right to free speech.

And while you're at it, get your Ham "ticket". Unlike the old days, there's no Morse code required, and a "Technician Class" license will give you access to a world of activist Patriots - at your fingertip. It takes about 4 hours to study for the exam, which takes 30 minutes to do. Then you can use two-way high-power radio transmitters in your car, you house, and hand-held "walkie-talkies". Using the local Ham repeaters, you can link into other amateur radio operators throughout the country and even around the world.

Chapter 4

Organizing Fellow Patriots into Community Activist Teams

You've gone to several local Tea Party meetings and have joined a 9/12 or other Patriot activist group. Good! Now it's time to spread the word. How about starting up your own group? It's time for all of us to become activist leaders, not passivist followers. Freedom is too precious. Multiply your efforts by planting a new seed of freedom like the legendary "Johnny Appleseed", the real John Chapman did as he worked his way across America in the early 19th century.

Make up some posters. Create a website. Think up a good group name, like: "RefoundingAmerica<yourcountyname>.com" or "MyLiberty<yourcountyname>.com". Check out *MyLibertySanMateo.com* for a real-world example of what one energized Patriot started in her spare time.

Set up a free e-mail account at *yahoo.com*. Find a local hall to meet. The local American Legion troop will have an auditorium. So will your local church, library or community center. You can often use the back room of a local restaurant which will be eager to provide you the facility for free - along with a few drinks and munchies sold to the participants. Contact all the groups mentioned in the previous Chapter. See our companion site *RefoundingAmericaBook.com* for lots of support materials including sample posters that you can download.

Create an agenda for the first meeting. The purpose of the group is to return America to its Constitutional founding, and to prevent the Progressives and Marxists from taking over the government and destroying our personal freedoms. Keep the meeting short, under 2 hours. Hold it at 6:30 PM to allow everyone to get there. Perhaps show a short DVD or YouTube clip to start off the event on an inspirational note. Check out *GlennBeck. com*, or *www.youtube.com/user/GlennBeckVideos* for short documentaries, to start. Schedule the next meeting for 2 weeks later.

Create an Individual Signup Sheet to get everyone involved. Ask for each person's name, e-mail and telephone number, and who their congressman is. Leave a line for what they'd most want to change. Leave an option for them to check a box if they would like to share their e-mail addresses with the other members of the group.

Then provide a check-off list of volunteer preferences. They could include:

- Contacting the Press & writing press releases

- Making signs, cards, fliers, brochures
- Developing publicity strategies
- Developing the Internet web site
- Acting as Treasurer for group meetings and activities
- Organizing fund raisers
- Handling outreach to other groups and political parties
- Organizing the agenda and event activities
- Manning tables & booths at fairs, plazas, malls
- Doing issues and candidate research (both supporting and opposing)
- Walking precincts to find new members and share the group's ideas and positions on candidates
- Making phone calls to support candidates
- Preparing government forms if the group decides to become a registered lobbying or recognized political activist organization (see RefoundingAmericaBook. com for how-to information on this).

As your group gets to know each other over the weeks, you will probably want to set up a book reading group which meets at one or more people's homes every few weeks.

You will also become closer to each of the other people and their families and will discover to your delight that you have a lot of new-found friends who have lots of the same values that you do concerning freedom, family, personal rights, responsibilities and the role of the government in our lives. Everyone will want to keep more in touch with everyone else.

Start having special Patriotic get-together meetings jut for fun. Cookouts are great. You can hold them in a public park or recreation center, or someone's back yard. Memorial Day, the Fourth of July, Veterans Day, Washington's Birthday, and other holidays come to mind. Everyone can invite their families. Everyone can bring some food to share.

At this point, you should circulate another Member signup sheet with name, address, telephone, e-mail, and a skills check-list. Skills (and business services) that someone has can be checked off. Skills that someone would like to learn could be circled. Here are some items:

- Printing (signs, banners, posters, cards)
- Graphic Arts & Design
- Web Design & Computer Programming
- Video & Film Making
- Photography
- Event Planning

- Library Skills
- Legal Services & Law
- Constitutional Law and History
- Election Law & Regulations
- Accounting & Bookkeeping Services
- Tax Preparation
- Publicity & PR,/Advertising
- Marketing
- Sales
- Political Polling & Market Research
- Catering & Cooking
- Firearms & Self Defense Training
- Electrical/Electrician/Solar Power
- Sheetrocking, roofing, framing, construction
- Plumbing & Heating
- Medical, Dental & Paramedic
- Automobile Bodywork & Repair
- Metalwork & Welding
- Woodwork & Carpentry
- Tractor & Truck Driving
- Farming & Gardening
- Canning & Food Preservation
- Amateur Radio
- LEO (sworn officer of the law)

Sharing skills are especially handy for group support during times of natural disasters and other emergencies. During times of emergencies, keeping track of friends and family is especially important. Earthquakes, floods, hurricanes, floods and fires call out for support. Creating a community of Patriots that can be there when the official community response might be overwhelmed or non-existent can make all the difference.

And in normal times, it's nice to be able to pay a friend for their professional services instead of a stranger. In close groups, inexpensive 5-watt handheld two-way portable radios can cover 3-to-5 miles or more when all other communications such as cell phone systems are temporarily out of order.   National retailers like Best Buy and Radio Shack carry lots of choices. And "Ham" handheld radio sets are even more flexible (a good way to get everyone in your group licensed with official call-signs).

Chapter 5

Making it Happen: Strategies for Activists

It's a good idea to recall two of Saul Alinsky's rules for radicals as we jump into specific ways to inform the public while entertaining your fellow Patriots. Rule Number 6 says that "a good tactic is one your people enjoy." Rule Number 5 acknowledges that "ridicule is man's most potent weapon." Both are true. Not only is it fun to make a serious point with humor; it usually drives your opponent crazy. People don't like to be laughed at. Too bad. The truth hurts – especially when it's funny.

Say you're retired and are outraged at the support your Representative or Senator is giving to nationalized health care. You don't want a bureaucratic "panel of experts" to decide whether to pay for your treatment or kick you to the curb with painkillers based on a preset chart. They may not call it a death panel, but refusing to grant a surgery or medication that would extend your life produces the same effect. Tell your member of Congress you don't agree with his or her position.

But remember, be funny. Instead of calling the district office, show up for an unannounced visit. Bring five to ten friends. If no one will talk to you, politely step outside on the sidewalk and lay down. Have a friend draw a white line around you with chalk. Get others to do the same. Make sure to get at least two people to hold signs reading, "This is a Die-In to Protest Congressional Death Panels," or "Seniors Have a Right to Life, Too." If you're feeling particularly saucy, dress up a member like the Grim Reaper wearing a name tag featuring the Representative or Senator's name. Of course, make sure to call the local media first so that your event is covered. If the press isn't there, it didn't happen.

Another way to spread your message is to find local businesses to partner with for a patriotic cause like the right to bear arms. Contact local firing ranges to set up an event for gun owners to come fire their weapons, enjoy a picnic, and exchange information. Put an announcement in your church bulletin, leave a flyer on your apartment's community board, or mention it to your child's scout leader. If you can confirm enough attendees, you may be able to negotiate a group discount.

Additionally, you may be surprised to find out that in states allowing guns to be carried openly, Starbucks provides a welcoming environment for gun owners who like to get caffeinated. As you will discover, there is a special pleasure that comes from ordering a double-latte while proudly displaying your favorite handgun. Mention this to your friends the next time you want to meet for coffee. Show your community that gun owners are not the kind of people to fear. Be friendly and cordial to the baristas, and pretty soon folks will get used to seeing guns being carried openly. We've experienced decades of Progressives flaunting their rights in public. Reverse the trend.

You've seen Progressives standing outside a business protesting. Yet, they always accuse their opponents as being the party, politicians, or movement of "NO!" Prove them wrong. Plan a "Support Fest." Pick a local or regional bank that did not take federal bailout money; either directly or indirectly through a parent company. Move your accounts into that bank. Then, contact the bank manager and schedule a "Support Fest" publicly thanking management for being prudent business people and free market patriots. Display signs like, "Thank You for Believing in the Free Market," and "I Bank with Capitalists, Not Cronies." Remember, call the media.

Of course, don't shy away from protesting. Just be more creative than Progressives. One of the icons of the Green movement is the Toyota Prius. In the early 2000s it became a status symbol for Progressives wanting to flash their eco-concern with a very distinctive car model. Unfortunately for Greenies, the Prius is not an environmentally friendly car. Yes, it uses less petroleum, but impacting the environment doesn't stop with reducing carbon emissions. The Prius' manufacturing process requires mining nickel from an area in Canada that has led to high levels of pollution and acid rain. Moreover, each step in the car's construction process requires the parts to be shipped from Canada to Europe, then China, before arriving in America. Total production cost per mile of a Prius? $3.25. Total for a Hummer? $1.95. Pay more, get less[1]. Now, *that's* progressive!

So, protest the Prius. Take up positions near a Toyota dealership, and hand out push cards directing people to CNW Marketing Research's commentary, "Hidden cost of driving a Prius." Encourage them to be environmentally friendly, but to do so with an eye towards winning them to your side. No one is pro-pollution, so point out how much the Prius pollutes the planet through its manufacturing process. We all agree that buying a product that creates acid rain doesn't make environmental sense. In fact, when it comes to building a Prius, it doesn't make economic sense either. If you want to be good to the Earth, buy a Hummer!

Hopefully, by now you're thinking of ways to modify these ideas into events and issues important to you. Part II discussed fifteen hot-button current issues. Go back now and see if you can find a way to take one of those topics and build a theme around it. Bonus points for humor!

Now, for some quick ideas to get you energized, and your group growing:

- Videotape elections with handheld cameras at polling stations in your area. Upload the videos to YouTube to expose any unusual activities, like bullying by hired thugs. See Part IV, the Toolbox, on using YouTube.

- Watch videos with family, friends, and neighbors. The documentary group, Citizens United, is an excellent resource for films that educate and entertain for liberty. See: *CitizensUnited.org*.

- Host a Patriot Block Party near or on state and national patriotic holidays, like the Fourth of July, Washington's Birthday, and Memorial Day. Invite the local TV stations.

- Start a Patriot Book Club. Studies show that you retain far more of the information you read, plus you'll have motivation to start and finish books that help you think more clearly, and debate more persuasively.

- Join at least one local 9/12 or Tea Party group. There are others just like you nearby. Find them. See Part V of the book for contact information. Hint: Our companion site RefoundingAmericaBook.com has lots of click-to information on TeaParty, 9/12 and other Patriot activist groups nationwide.

- Order pocket sized copies of the combined Declaration of Independence and Constitution from the CATO Institute. Carry it with you at all times, and share it whenever you get a chance to. Activism starts with this one small step.

- Download David Horowitz's Rule for Revolutionaries for free from our companion site *RefoundingAmericaBook.com*. Read it and follow them.

- Set up five screen names. Reply to progressive online media companies and blogs every day to five different websites. Keep to your values, and show the editors that their writers are out of sync with their readership. If 100,000 readers of this book reply to 5 progressive sites daily, we'll have 3 1/2 million opportunities to refute their lies and spread the truth to 100 times more readers every week. And the press follows these progressive sites...

- Reply to a progressive/mainstream media poll at least once a week. Places like MSNBC, CNN, and all the networks frequently solicit input from the public for the polling data they report. Let your voice be heard and make a difference. Call their 800 numbers, answer their web polls - and vote!

- Send at least one letter to the editor of a major local newspaper each month via email. Adhere strictly to the word limit. Be accurate and memorable. Highlight topics in the news, either the issues themselves or how the news is covering them. For a free list of the e-mails of the editors of the major newspapers throughout the country, go to *RefoundingAmericaBook.com*.

- Check the opinion column submission guidelines for all local newspapers. Many are eager to print "man on the street" pieces from people living in their circulation area. You probably won't get paid, but if your work is well done, you may be able to arrange a regular column to spread patriotic ideas! Especially eager for local content are the free local "shopper" papers like Examiner.com. And the Examiner group is a friendly anti-Progressive voice.

- Join patriot-friendly groups with local meetings and a national presence. One great example is the state and local chapter of the National Rifle Association.

- Also consider joining the mailing lists of several free market think tanks, like the Heritage Foundation and the Heartland Institute. Part V of this book provides the names of websites of all the major national and state free market think tanks. They are excellent resources for up-to-date research and iron-clad talking points. Government officials and talking heads use the information these groups produce – why not you?

- Volunteer to man a telephone bank from home to call potential voters on behalf of candidates throughout the country. Technology makes it possible for ideologically similar people to assist one another across the country in real time. Scott Brown's victory in Massachusetts got a tremendous boost from like-minded phone bankers willing to pick up a phone and make a few calls.

- Donate to a patriotic candidate's campaign via his or her website. Groups like the Independence Caucus (*icaucus.org*) and Campaign for Liberty (CampaignForLiberty.com) provide terrific direction on which candidates possess a constitutionalist's understanding of our government.

- Picket your local TV stations. Create signs supporting Freedom of Speech and against government control of the airwaves and Internet. Argue against National ID cards and excessive military installations overseas. Call for "People's Rights" to their own bodies not just woman's rights. Call for privacy and the end of Big Brother. These are hot-button "civil rights" issues of the Progressives who are TV journalists. Then counter-punch with signs calling for Bill of Rights and the Constitution. Be bold and audacious. Call to "Stop discrimination against Honkeys" (a pejorative word for middle class white people used by many Progressives).

- Do a Constitutional Give-Away. Get a bunch of Pocket Constitutions & Declarations of Independence from *Heritage.org, Cato.org* or *ACRU.org.* or download your own from the RefoundingAmericaBook.com website and print them out.[2] Make up some signs listing the Bill of Rights saying "Free" and "Take One". Give away the Booklets at your local malls. Ask the people who take one if they'd like to learn more about your group and the ideas of liberty and freedom that you stand for, and get their name and e-mail address. Take a large American Flag with you.

[1]Go to: http://www.cnwmr.com/nss-folder/automotiveenergy/Hidden%20Cost%20of%20Driving%20a%20Prius%20Commentary.pdf

[2]For Refounding American Book Insiders, a free copy can be ordered from CATO by using the special code included on the back of this book. See the Refounding America Book website for more details.

Chapter 6

Capturing the Media's Attention - And Your Neighbor's

Get yourself on a local talk show

Call in to the host as a regular member of the public, or obtain an interview as a local Patriot activist group. Talk about your group and what you plan to do. Here are some tips, courtesy of Ron Paul's CampaignFor-Liberty.org:

1. What you should know

When calling a talk radio program, only pick one or two talking points to say. It is best to relate them to a topic already being discussed on the program. Be kind and respectful to the call-screener and the host.

When you get on the air, try not to talk too much or allow the host to get you "off topic." Make your point quickly and then wait for the host to respond. After the host responds, make your second point and then finish the call. This is the best time to mention your group. If you support a particular national organization like *Campaign For Liberty*, then end by saying something like, "that's why I support *Campaign for Liberty*."

While you may only have time to make one or two points during a phone call, many hosts will likely ask you what your group or campaign is about; be prepared by asking yourself the same question.

Be committed to educating your family, friends, and neighbors about the limited government philosophy. Point out that your group is working on the local, state, and federal levels to stop unconstitutional and corrosive legislation while promoting bills that secure our rights, and candidates who agree with these values.

Invite the audience to contact your group via your web site. Point out that your goal is to advance the cause of freedom in your local area. The battle to take back our nation begins in our own backyard!

* Your mission is to promote and defend the great American principles of individual liberty, constitutional government, sound money, free markets, and a noninterventionist foreign policy, by means of educational and political activity.

2. Suggested Talking Points

Economy:

* The congressional pay raise scheduled to automatically take place in 2010 should not be allowed to go through. They should have to cut back and sacrifice just like their constituents.

* During these tough economic times, stopping the pay raise would show that Washington is serious about fiscal responsibility.

* At the very least, a vote should be taken instead of allowing the raise to automatically happen. The Obama administration should welcome this move to increase transparency and accountability.

* After decades of deficit spending and unconstitutional entitlement programs, each American's individual share of the federal government's liabilities is now $184,000... and rising. The current budget deficit is more

than at any other time in history. This happened under a so-called conservative president/congress. We have to find our way again.

* Economic freedom is based on a simple rule: everyone has the right to his or her life and property.

* In the United States, many citizens seek to use the government to enrich themselves at their neighbors' expense. This is immoral. We should stop using the government to do things that would be considered morally outrageous if done by a private individual. It is a shame that a Republican administration that was backed by conservatives presided over one of the biggest thefts in history: the bailout of the banks and automotive industry. We have to find our way back to fiscal sanity before we can dream of winning an election.

* Why would we expect a system based on legal theft, as ours is, to be a net benefit to the poor or middle class? Every one of the special benefits that have been enacted by both Republicans and Democrats makes companies less efficient and competitive, and the economy more sluggish. This is exactly what will happen with Bush's bailouts and Obama's social spending.

* There should be no income tax, national sales tax, or any other such scheme on the federal level. The US income tax implies that government owns you and graciously allows you to keep whatever percentage of the fruits of your labor it chooses. This is incompatible with the principles of a free society.

* Conservatives criticized Obama for having a lavishly expensive inauguration amidst a time of economic hardship for America. But these millions of dollars are nothing compared to the billions and trillions squandered by both parties in the last decade. It seems like targeting the inauguration is an easy way for people to sound fiscally conservative while ignoring what's really bankrupting the taxpayer: too much government spending and debt.

* Elected Republicans are sounding more financially prudent every day, now that they have lost Congress and the presidency. But let us remember how spendthrift they were in power. For talk about fiscal restraint to be anything more than a way to score partisan points, we as a people need to rethink the role of government on a fundamental level.

* Obama claims the issue is not big government vs. small government, but making government work. Well, most elected Republicans have surely abandoned any role as the party of small government, so, tragically, he might have a point. Obama also says programs that don't work will be eliminated. I'll believe it when I see it: almost never does anyone from either party eliminate a government program.

Foreign Policy:

* We can't expect to have a limited government at home while we have an interventionist foreign policy abroad. The two are intertwined, as the Bush Administration's 8 years have shown us. If we truly want limited government, then we need to stop policing the world.

* Our fighting men and women are stationed on over 700 bases in more than 100 countries. It is time to bring them home to protect our own country instead of focusing on guarding other nations.

* The war on terror has awakened more Americans than ever to the way government exploits fear, and even its own failures, to justify eroding civil liberties. You cannot have limited government at home while having a big-government foreign policy. The Bush Administration and willing conservatives presided over the largest increase in government because they forgot this reality.

* A strong national defense doesn't mean policing the world, launching preemptive war, or having troops stationed on every continent. Those things weaken our national defense by spreading our resources too thin and bankrupting our government at home.

* Hopefully, conservatives will now recognize that government has limits in foreign policy as well as domestic.

* Obama promises to expand the war in Afghanistan. It has been a nation-building disaster for seven years, and I have little hope he will turn it around. He has already begun to show force against Pakistan. So much for the anti-war candidate.

* Republicans talked as though the commander-in-chief could do no wrong when Bush was in power. I hope they realize they were wrong and dissent from Obama's foreign policy when they believe it is not in the nation's interests.

<u>Civil Liberties:</u>

* Freedom means not only that our economic activity ought to be free and voluntary, but that government should stay out of our personal affairs as well. Freedom means that we understand liberty as an indivisible whole. The government should stay out of our wallets, out of our privacy, out of the way we educate our kids, and out of our lives.

* Government should respect our right to privacy, rather than invading it on phony pretenses. Instead of trying to correct our bad habits at the point of a gun, it should defer to families and the normal channels of civil society to instruct people on moral conduct.

* Bush amassed great power during his presidency, and now the Democrats have it. Those who cheered him on are partly to blame for whatever Obama does to invade our privacy, our finances, and our liberties.

Write letters to the editor

Another way to make your point is to write a steady stream of letters to the editor of your local newspaper. Keep the letters short and punchy so that yours will stand out. Don't be afraid to saturate the editor's desk with your opinions. One benefit is that the quality of your letters will improve the more you write. Another is becoming a regular contributor to the "Letters to the Editor" page so that others in the community will recognize your name and your viewpoint. Pretty soon, you'll be able to turn that name recognition into a brand that attracts other patriot activists to your cause. So, grab a pen or keyboard and get going!

 Be sure to go to the www.RefoundingAmericaBook.com website for free contact information for America's top newspaper editors!

Chapter 7
Winning Elections in 2010: How We the People Will Win

David Horowitz is a genius. Raised by two Communist parents and himself a sworn died-in-the-wool 60's radical anarchist, he was intimately involved with his Marxist brethren who plotted the overthrow of the United States. Some, like members of the Weather Underground, used bombs and bullets to promote their twisted idea of Utopia. Other Marxists lowered their visibility and crawled underground to ingratiate themselves with liberal-thinkers. All of them survived to grow up and live to fight another day. They were swept into power when the Obama Progressive machine took over in the fall of 2008. That day has now arrived.

David Horowitz was very lucky. While still a young man, he was able to see the corrupt and shallow arguments that his fellow-anarchists made. He broke free of his Marxist bonds and has spent the rest of his life arguing for freedom and liberty and the right of the individual against the totalitarian mindset of the Progressives. It has nearly cost him his life on several occasions. He gets serious death threats weekly by the "lefties", as he alls them.

David Horowitz is a real Patriot. His expose-the-Marxist website is: *DiscovertheNetworks.org*, is a guide to the political left where he connects the dots showing how all the Progressive/Marxist organizations and people are linked together. If you want to know who the enemy is, check here first.

The HorowitzFreedomCenter.org is the flagship institution created to fight the Progressives. Here there are links to JihadWatch.org and the insidious relationship between Progressives and radical Muslim terrorists. *FrontPageMag.com* is his news site which provides day-by-day information on what the Progressives and their "freedom-hating friends" are doing.

David has observed that the Art of Politics is the Art of War. He says to "invert the paradigm" by doing - with humor - what the radical leftists do with hate. Hold "death-ins", "tax-ins", "green-ins". Use the Saul Alinsky tactics in a friendly way to make fun of the Progressives - and be sure to get local press and TV coverage in the process.

He has spelled out the six principles the Patriot activist must learn to win the battle for freedom. He points out that the left already understands these principles well, and uses them daily.

Follow these six simple principles and we the people will win. They are the key to winning the battle of the hearts and minds of the undecided, the confused, the Independent voter, the fed-up Democrat, the RINO Republican in Name Only.

1) Politics is War conducted by other means

Progressives conduct their political campaigns as a form of warfare. They play tackle football while conservatives usually play touch football. "In political warfare you do not fight just to prevail in an argument, but to destroy the enemy's fighting position". Winning - as understood by the audience - does not depend on scoring logical points but on making emotional points - in sound bites. Watch the national TV political shows. You get 30 seconds to make your point. Any longer, and you lose.   You have to get the first punch in.

You have to paint your Progressive enemy as a narcissistic power-mad, mean-spirited, government control freak; a corrupt Marxist elitist in the pockets of ruthless billionaires like George Soros whose policies are keeping minority people poor and dependent and slaves to their government masters.   If you don't attack first, he will call you a border-line racist controlled by religious bible-thumping zealots. Get it? He who throws the second punch loses. And every one of these statements describing the Progressive-Marxist is true. You are telling the truth. Your enemy is telling lies.

2) Politics is a War of Position

In any war there are only two sides. You are either a friend or an enemy. Don't get confused. Your job is to describe yourself as the friend of as large a constituency as possible. Define your opponent as the enemy of that group.

You are for motherhood, your enemy is against motherhood. You believe in God, your enemy hates God and is an Atheist. You are for personal privacy. Your enemy wants National ID cards and government snooping. You are for personal charity and generous giving by every individual out of love and compassion for the needy. Your enemy is in favor of government force in taking away people's wealth to squander it on its corrupt sycophants. And always, you are for the cause of the underdog and the Progressive enemy is the oppressor and victimizer.

As in military battles, choosing the right terrain is important. Select one that stacks the battle in your favor. Remember when President Obama argued for his Big-Government Health Care Bill on the White House lawn - surrounded by doctors wearing white coats (the "good guys"). Those weren't the doctors own jackets. A White House staffer handed them and said "put these on" just before the TV cameras started broadcasting.

3) In Political War, the Aggressor usually wins

Never wait for the other side to attack first. This is called a "prevent defense" in football. It's called "losing" in politics. You often get only one chance. Since position is a war of position, being aggressive is advantageous. Images stick in the mind of the viewer. When you strike first, you are the one who set's the agenda and the issues. Your opponent must respond to your question. And if he doesn't answer your point, then in the second round call him on it and remind the audience that he's slippery and dishonest and can't even answer the question asked. Defining the opposition is the decisive move in all political war.

Note: pay particular care as to how negatively you want to paint your Progressive opponent. You must smear him with some of his Marxist goop, but too strong a negative position can cause an underdog backlash in the observer's mind, and you never want a power-mad Progressive to be seen as an underdog. Loser yes, underdog no.

4) Power is defined by Fear and Hope

Fear and Hope are the flip sides of the political coins. If you provide people with hope, they will be your friend. Remember "Hope and Change" was the Progressive slogan in 2008. Few listeners who swooned to these words understood they really meant loss of freedom and serfdom for themselves - and power to their soon-to-be elitist masters. Never inspire fear. You will make enemies.

It's easy for a Patriot to show hope. Show them that your way really is the way of hope - for a better future and a return to the Constitution and its founding principles. Since you know your Progressive enemy is going to try to paint you as bigoted and intolerant, focus your opening position as inclusive and fair-minded. Smile and lead with images that show charity, generosity and love.

You can also show that your Progressive opponent is full of fear and distrust for the individual. He really wants to control and regulate every aspect of their lives, how much water their toilet can hold, what kind of light bulbs they must use, and so on. He thinks they are too stupid to take care of themselves so he wants to create a Nanny State with Big Brother's fist to force compliance. And with him in control.

It should be easy to make a listener very very afraid of a Progressive

Marxist state. Remind them of Stalin and Hitler's love of "progressive" ideas like euthanasia (killing old people) and forced sterilization of "dumb people" and abortion (killing the unborn). These were all wildly popular Progressive ideas the turn of the 20th century.

5) The Weapons of Politics are symbols evoking Fear and Hope
Conservatives lose the battle when they come across as scolding, scowling and sanctimonious. Always be the opposite. You care about people as individuals. You live the Golden Rule in your own life, you are generous and loving and kind and treat other people as you would like to be treated. Do the same thing in your battle with the Progressive opponent.

Remember too that you only have a short sound bite. Speak loudly and clearly is a strong, friendly and happy voice. Laugh. "Keep it simple and keep it short". Create a slogan. People remember slogans. Repeat it again and again.

Get on local TV whenever possible. TV is far more important than radio. As David Horowitz points out: "in politics, television is reality". Focus on your short sound-bite message and repeat it over and over. "Images - symbols and sound-bites - will always prevail", before they cut away to the commercial. Focus only on one or two points, no more than three. Too many and your entire message will be lost.

Progressives have a "party line". It's been around for a very long time, since Marx invented Communism. During a legislative battle, whenever a Progressive steps in front of a camera, he always has at least one line in his speech that another colleague will also repeat over and over. Like: "tax breaks are for the wealthy at the expense of the poor". It's a lie and you know it, but if it's repeated over and over - especially by different people -then the lie will somehow seem to be true. Repetition works in television commercials. It works in political speeches too.

Always march to the tune of the same drummer when you are joining forces with other Patriots. Sync up your speeches and discussion points and slogans before hand. Be prepared. Your up against pros whose playbook is over 150 years old and counts 90 million murdered as its success.

Symbols, slogans and sound bites determine votes. Carefully choose your words and phrases. They are more important than party platforms, manifestos and speeches. You are your image. Your image is what you project.

6) Victory lies on the side of the People

Each of the principles has a bottom line. You must first define yourself in ways that the average person can immediately understand. You must give the people hope - hope that you will win. You must give the people fear - fear that your Progressive opponent will win. Identify yourself and your issues as helping the victim and the underdog, the minorities, the disadvantaged. Identify yourself with the regular guy, the ordinary Joe and regular Jane. As David Horowitz points out this is what every lying Progressive statement says: "we care about women, children, minorities, working Americans and the poor". Then: "Conservatives are mean-spirited, serve the rich and don't care about you". You and I know that these are lies but Progressives have no problem staring you straight in the face and lying to you. It's a pathological behavior shared by all narcissists and psychopaths.

You must make your campaign a cause. During the Cold War, Conservatives had a clear-cut cause: saving America from Communism. This cause was deeply understood by the American people. Even the poorest person understood that their very freedom was at stake. Conservatives were elected to defend the country. Today's battle against the Progressives is simply a continuation of the Cold War, except the battle is against the totalitarian left at home as well as abroad.

The sadistic dictator Stalin said; ""America is like a healthy body and its resistance is threefold: its patriotism, its morality and its spiritual life. If we can undermine these three areas, America will collapse from within." The Progressives are against Patriotism (ever see one proud to wear an American Flag lapel pin?). They are against Morality (euthanasia, government-sponsored abortion) and are where most of the Atheists can be found. The campaign against the Progressive dogma is a campaign against the totalitarianism of the Marxist dictator.

PART IV: THE TOOL BOX

"I don't make jokes. I just watch the government and report the facts."
-Will Rogers

Every craftsman needs a tool box. In the following twelve chapters we lay out the tools necessary for taking your message beyond your local community via the world wide web. Modern technology offers an array of outlets for Patriots looking for like-minded souls. If you've never worked a website or written a blog, don't worry. We've taken the guesswork out by including easy-to-follow, step-by-step processes for creating and using every form of multimedia in this part of the book. We've even included screen shots of each page so you can follow along in front of your computer. Let's go!

Chapter 1 shows you how to create a website using one of the many popular free webhosting services on the internet. It also names two of the most helpful domain name directories allowing you to search for and reserve a name for your website.

Chapter 2 introduces the explosively popular tool of blogging. The more widely read your blog becomes, the more it can influence other blogs through links to your material.

Chapter 3 presents two online resources for communicating electronically with members of Congress. Great for individuals and groups!

Chapter 4 gives the skinny on faxes. Like emails, faxes can be used to communicate with politicians; especially to show support or opposition in a flurry.

Chapter 5 provides links to the telephone numbers for House and Senate members of the 111th Congress.

Chapter 6 shares links to the telephone numbers for the top 100 broadcast television markets in the country.

Chapter 7 walks you through the process of setting up a YouTube account.

Chapter 8 does the same for uStream.tv.

Chapter 9 covers the most popular social networking sites, like Facebook, MySpace, Twitter, and Meetup.

Chapter 10 directs you where to go to get the most up-to-date media contact lists, including telephone numbers, email addresses, and physical addresses.

Chapter 11 offers links to internet companies that specialize in custom political advertising.

Chapter 12 provides resources for setting up a Political Action Committee (PAC).

Chapter 1

The Website

So you want to start a website. What to do? First, decide on a name and see if it is already in use by checking the domain name registry. *NetworkSolutions.com* and *Verio.com*, among others, are companies that provide easy ways to search for website (i.e. domain) names that have not been registered, and are thus available. The name should be something catchy that helps people to identify the kind of content available on the site. Ideally, it will contain words that attract a search engine's attention when other patriot-activists are looking for information or people that interest them. Once you find an available name, you can reserve/register the name for a fee.

Next, you'll need to decide how to "host" your website. In order for people to visit and use your website, it must be connected to the internet. Since most people don't have the financial capacity to personally own a server large enough to handle internet traffic, they use "web-hosting" companies. Some are free, others charge a fee.

Among websites that offer quick start registration, templates, and free hosting are *Weebly.com, Wix.com*, and *Sites.Google.com*. All three provide readymade website templates, plus drag-and-drop add-on features like pictures, maps, text, and videos. In exchange for not charging to host a website, some hosts run advertisements to attract revenue. Others restrict bandwidth, storage, or page numbers with upgrades available for subscribing to a monthly fee. In addition, paying a fee usually drops the host's name from the domain name. (E.g. example.com instead of example.wix. com)

http://computer.howstuffworks.com/web-page.htm

http://www.weebly.com/

http://www.wix.com/

http://sites.google.com/

Network Solutions provides three different services for registering a domain name. The first is searching for a new, available name. This service searches for all possible types of names and extensions, including .com, .org, .edu, .net, .tv, and many more – even in other coutries!

The second service helps you to generate a domain name. Since a successful domain name both attracts and informs people about your site's purpose, plugging in key words helps Network Solutions select the domain names that best reflect that purpose.

Finally, Network Solutions helps you obtain the domain name you want from others if it's already taken.

Another helpful domain name registry website is Verio. Verio also provides a searchable database for domain names and extensions. In addition, it lets you filter explicit language suggestions, and expand your results to include hyphenated domain names.

Note: Both Network Solutions and Verio offer subscription-based webhosting for websites using the domain name you register. Each company's webhosting service can be purchased as a bundle when registering your domain name, or separately.

An example of a company that provides free webhosting is Weebly. The following is a step-by-step process for signing up for free webhosting from Weebly.

First, go to *www.weebly.com*, and click the orange "Sign Up" button.

Next, enter the domain name of your website. If you already own a domain name, choose Option C. If you don't and want free Weebly webhosting, choose Option A for a *.weebly.com* account. If you don't and don't want .weebly in your domain name, choose Option B to create a subscription for Weebly webhosting. After choosing one of the three options, click the orange "Continue" button.

You are now at the Desktop where you can create a personalized website. Weebly makes adding features to your webpage easy by allowing you to drag-and-drop them into your webpage.

The tabs near the top left side of the screen allow you to view and select page elements, design layouts, how to manage the number and types of your pages, and your website's settings.

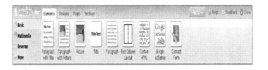

Once you are finished selecting your features and settings, click the orange "Publish" button near the top right side of the webpage. You are now on the World Wide Web!

Chapter 2

The Blog

Much of the same advice applies to starting a blog as with starting a website. Some of the most popular free blog-hosts are Blogger, LiveJournal, and Xanga. Like Weebly, these websites allow users to publish online within minutes of creating an account. For bloggers with more tech savvy, WordPress and Movable Type are open source (i.e. free, constantly improving) software programs that give individual users much more creative control over the look and feel of the blog. Additionally, the blog's website address is not identified as domainname.blogger, or domainname.xanga. However, WordPress and Movable Type users must secure independent web-hosting in order to run either program.

Once you are up and running, there are important considerations to keep in mind if you want to attract and increase your readership. First, you must be consistent both in style and timeliness. Like the great op-ed writers, bloggers gain market share with a reliable point of view delivered in a personally unique way. Since news and commentary cycles quicken every day, you must commit to blogging several times a week to keep readers interested and aware of your opinions. The need to consume and comment on the news on a daily (or near daily) basis leads many bloggers to search for ways to make money from their blogging.

Like print publications, the vast majority of money-making blogs rely on some type of advertising revenue to make a profit. There are several models. One is to link to other websites on your blog roll (i.e. a list of other blogs or sites provided on your main page) for a fee. BlogRollPlease.com offers such an arrangement. Other means of producing money include setting up relationships with advertising sites like AdSense, Google Ad Words, Amazon, or any number of other affiliates. There are a range of options depending on the level of income you are trying to generate from blogging.

The second key is to develop an expertise. Most bloggers fall into one of two categories: reporters or experts. Reporters tend to aggregate information about a topic and describe what people are saying about it. Experts are people who are doing the saying. Becoming an expert has two benefits for bloggers. On the one hand it gives your readers an opinion informed by knowledge and experience. On the other, it helps to focus your energies on a much smaller issue set, thus allowing you to carve out a niche within the larger blogging community. As with most sectors of today's economy, it is vital that you specialize in a specific area to maximize your effort and impact as a must-read blogger.

http://computer.howstuffworks.com/internet/social-networking/information/blog.htm

http://www.blogrollplease.com/sell-blogroll-links.php

http://www.problogger.net/archives/2009/12/16/how-to-make-30000-a-year-blogging/

Here is a step-by-step process – with screenshots! – showing you how to set up a blog account with Blogger. com, a free and popular blog hosting website. Note: Since Google owns Blogger, you'll need to create a free Google account in order to set up a free Blogger account. The upshot is that you'll be able to use your Username and Password on the full spectrum of Google products, including Gmail.

So first, go to *www. blogger.com.* Click on the orange button that says, "Create a Blog".

Next, create a Google account by providing the required information. When you are finished, click "Continue" at the bottom.

Then, name your blog. Pick something that is memorable, yet difficult to make fun of. Ideally, your blog's name will connect readers to your blog's purpose. For example, National Review Online hosts a blog called "The Campaign Spot" that serves as the primary discussion place for campaign-related news and commentary. After confirming that your chosen name is available, click "Continue".

Finally, choose a template from Blogger, or create your own. If you're itching to get started choose a template and modify or replace it later. The world needs to know your thoughts! When you select a template, click "Continue".

You're finished! Now you can start blogging and building your readership, expertise, and influence. Invite friends to read and comment – or even contribute. Add other blogs you like to your Blog Roll, and ask if they will return the favor. Be consistent and insightful. The internet if your playground!

Once you log in, you'll be prompted (and tempted) to write something. Go ahead. Write whatever you want; include photos, text, and hyperlinks to other web-based information. Make sure to fill in the Title and Labels sections so readers can categorize your content. If you want to change something, you can edit before, during, after posting. Also, the tabs at the top let you navigate around your blog so you can personalize the look and feel of your blog.

Chapter 3

Email

Congress.org allows registrants to send emails or printed letters to members of Congress, Senate, President, and all governors and state legislators free of charge. The website is easy to navigate and it gives registrants the ability to post comments about issues, as well as receive free weekly updates on member-specific voting records. Advocacy groups can contract for enhanced emailing or letter delivery services for a fee.

http://www.congress.org/

CongressMerge.com (via *Grassfire.com*) provides subscription services for personal contact information for US House and Senate members that are regularly updated.

http://www.congressmerge.com/products/index.htm

Chapter 4

Faxes

Though used less frequently than other forms of electronic communication like email or texting, faxes continue to be a method of communication with elected officials. The key to remember when faxing is to make your letter as close to one page as possible to increase the chance of it being read. Moreover, avoid sending mass copies of the same fax to the same politician because many will opt to ignore them. Be original, and the chances of someone actually reading your message dramatically increase.

*FreedomSpeaks.com is a free service allowing people to send emails and faxes to elected officials. The website makes its money by selling demographic data of its users and charging politicians a fee for sharing their contact information.

http://www.freedomspeaks.com/default.aspx

*Grassfire.com provides personal telephone and fax numbers for US House and Senate members. Users can either use the information to send their own faxes, or pay Grassfire a fee to schedule personalized faxes to a smaller number of key elected officials. In addition, Grassfire hosts petitions for signatures that are then sent to elected officials.

http://www.grassfire.com/

Chapter 5

Phone

Telephone numbers for members of the current (i.e. 111th) Congress are available from the House Clerk's office in a PDF file.

http://clerk.house.gov/member_info/ttd_111.pdf

Telephone numbers for individual United States Senators can also be accessed via PDF file.

http://clerk.house.gov/member_info/senators.pdf

Chapter 6

Radio/TV

*NewsLink.org provides a listing for each news talk radio station grouped by state and city.

http://www.newslink.org/rneradi.html

*StationIndex.com provides a comprehensive listing of the Top 100 Television Markets, with individual listings of every major television station located within each market, including a hyperlink to the station's website.

http://www.stationindex.com/tv/tv-markets

Chapter 7

YouTube

If you want to make an instant impact through an online video, becoming a member of YouTube is a must. While you don't need an account to watch videos posted to YouTube, you will need to create one if you intend to post videos or comments. Posting videos on YouTube begins by creating a free account. Once registered, users can immediately begin to upload original content from their computer onto the site. For basic users, videos are limited to 1 GB in size and 10 minutes in length.

For beginners, the YouTube Handbook is an excellent resource for tips on lighting, camera, and sound techniques, as well as advice on uploading videos and creating special effects. Another helpful website is Videomaker.com, which contains a multitude of how-to articles and videos free of charge. YouTube also hosts a "Creators Corner" page that helps aspiring videographers think up projects, optimize videos for YouTube, and connect to other users.

http://money.howstuffworks.com/youtube.htm
http://www.youtube.com/
http://www.youtube.com/t/yt_handbook_produce
http://www.videomaker.com/

The following is a step-by-step process for creating a YouTube account, and uploading video.

To create a YouTube account, click on "Create Account" in the upper right corner of the YouTube homepage.

Fill in the requested information boxes, and click the "I Accept" button acknowledging you agree with the terms of service for using YouTube.

Like many other mainstream websites, getting started with YouTube is easier when you already have – or are willing to create – a Google account. Through strategic partnerships or outright ownership, Google is connected to a lot of other companies.

This includes YouTube, which Google owns. If you already have a Google account, sign in to create your YouTube account by entering your information in the left column. If not, create one by entering the requested information in the right column.

You are now registered with YouTube and ready to begin broadcasting yourself! If you like, you can subscribe to friends who are already on YouTube. If you want to begin broadcasting, start by clicking the yellow "Upload" button in the top right corner.

The process for uploading video is very similar to uploading an attachment to an email. Clicking on the "Upload Video" button near the upper middle of the page will allow you to access videos from your computer.

Just underneath the "Upload Video" button are links to help you connect your Facebook, Twitter, and Google Reader accounts to YouTube so that a post on YouTube will simultaneously post to these other accounts.

Finally, the column on the right side gives helpful advice on avoiding copyright infringement when uploading videos.

After selecting a video, picture, or PowerPoint presentation to upload and clicking on it, you will receive confirmation that it was successfully uploaded.

After your video upload is successful, type in a name, description, and tags (i.e. word or phrases) so other people searching for videos like yours kind find it. Then click "Save Changes" near the bottom left. Next, click "Go To My Videos", so you can be transported to a listing of the videos you've uploaded. Once there, you can play, edit, and share your video. When you're done, it's time to create another video!

Chapter 8

UStream.tv

Ustream allows users to broadcast themselves live over the internet within two minutes of creating a free account. All you need is an internet connection and an attached video camera. The broadcast allows viewers on both sides to interact with each other, similar to a video conference, but with much greater clarity.

http://www.ustream.tv/

http://www.ustream.tv/get-started

All you need to begin broadcasting on Ustream is a computer, internet connection, microphone, and a webcam or video camera. Ustream's system will automatically detect your camera type. Thereafter, starting a new show takes only as long as creating a username and password; clicking on "Your Shows"; typing the name of your show in the "Create New Show" box, followed by clicking "Create". Then, click "Broadcast Now". Once you click "Allow" giving permission for Ustream to access your webcam or camera, you'll be broadcasting! The following pages are a step-by-step process from creating an account to broadcasting a show.

Signing up is easy if you already have a Google or Yahoo account Username and Password. If not, you can input the requested information in less than a minute.

After signing in, create a Username and Password that you can easily remember.

Then, complete the information prompts to fill-out your profile settings.

If you like, you can import contacts from your email account, or connect your Twitter account to send alerts to your friends and followers. If not, skip it.

Now, you're ready to start your free, live broadcast! Under the "Your Shows" tab, create a name for your first video and click "Broadcast Now".

Then, create a name for your show, upload a logo, select a category for people to search, include some tags (i.e. words or phrases that people can search), and write up a brief description. All of these will help others find you.

Click the green icon "Broadcast Now". You will be prompted to allow access to your camera and microphone. Click "Allow Access" to begin broadcasting. When you do, you will be greeted by the following screen.

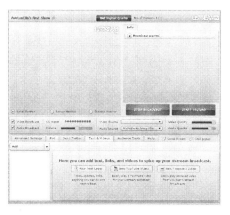

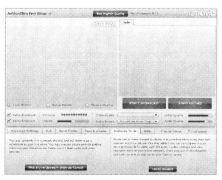

When you are ready, click either "Start Broadcast" to begin a live feed, or "Start Record" to create a file to broadcast later. Both options will provide you ways to end or edit your audio and video as you see fit.

Additionally, clicking the tabs at the bottom of the screen enables you to enhance your broadcast by importing YouTube videos, Twitter feeds, audience polling so you'll know who is watching, among others tools. The "Audience Tools" tab allows you to pick a live Ustream show to co-host, or invite other Ustream users to watch your video.

You can also manage your account by clicking on the "Dashboard" tab back at your main profile page. Doing so allows you to see which feeds you are monitoring, and whether you want to add, delete, or modify the broadcasts that interest you.

Chapter 9

Social Networking:
Facebook, Twitter, Myspace, Ning, Meetup

FACEBOOK: Although originally designed as a social networking site for college students, Facebook has since expanded to allow anyone to join, so long as they provide a valid email address, and answer background questions about schools attended and work histories. Facebook then creates a standardized profile that users can modify. The profile is searchable by other Facebook users, with limited searching and viewing allowed to non-members on the internet. The biggest advantage to Facebook is a consistent design and easy-to-use navigation tools.

http://www.facebook.com/

The following is a step-by-step guide to creating a Facebook account. First, go to the homepage and fill in the information boxes.

Step 1 prompts you to allow Facebook to access your email address book by giving it your password. This allows Facebook to find your friends who are already Facebook members and connect you to them. If you prefer to find them yourself, click "Skip this step" at the bottom right corner.

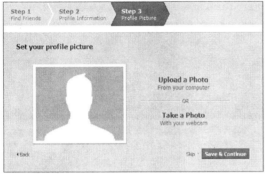

Step 2 will prompt you to provide information about high schools and colleges attended; again, in order to connect you to networks that will help you find others who attended the same schools. You can also skip this step by clicking on those words at the bottom right corner.

Step 3 allows you to upload a profile picture from your computer, or to take a snapshot from a webcam. This step can also be skipped.

After completing Steps 1-3, confirm your Facebook account by checking the email account you provided. Open the email from Facebook and click on the link provided to finish the account creation process. The link will take you to your completed Facebook account.

Click on the "Profile" tab at the top of the page to go to your new, main Facebook page! Once there complete the informational data requested so that people will know who you are, what you stand for, and what interests you. The column on the left lets you search for friends and groups that speak to your issues. Enjoy!

MYSPACE: MySpace is a social networking site that provides a highly customizable experience for its users. Similar to other sites, registrants can upload pictures, videos, music, and web addresses to personalize their pages. They can also search for other users via an internal search engine.

http://www.myspace.com/

MySpace allows potential users to peruse the website before signing up via the "Take a Tour" link near the top left corner of the page, just to the right of the MySpace logo.

The information on the other side of the link provides the same type of information as an "About Us" section found on websites of all kinds. Once you decide to create an account, click the "Sign Up" button near the bottom.

Then, fill in the requested information in the boxes provided.

Next, if you enter a Google Gmail account for your email address, MySpace asks for your password in order to search for friends from your address book that are already on MySpace. If you do not want to share your password, click the words "skip this step" to the right of the button "Find Friends".

You will then be prompted to confirm the creation of your MySpace accout by accessing the email account you provided. Open the email from MySpace and click on the link confirming your account.

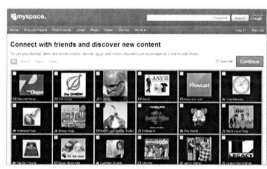

The link takes you back to MySpace to begin building your networks of friends and interests. Click the pink "Continue" button near the top right corner to continue personalizing your profile.

MySpace then prompts you to upload a profile picture, or take a snapshot with a webcam. You can also skip this step.

Next, you can add the schools you've attended so you'll be connected to former classmates automatically.

Finally, you can include your city, state, and postal code to allow others to find you easier.

You are now ready to use your MySpace page!

NING: This social networking tool enables users to create a website that is easily and personally customizable. Administrators of Ning Networks can set up a range of features including blogs for every member, message boards, commenting, online chats, video and photo applications, plus event planning and notification. Several 9/12 inspired groups use Ning Networks to attract, organize, and educate like-minded patriot activists.

http://about.ning.com/product.php

Ning is a webhosting company that targets users who want to create social networking websites. Like other free webhosting companies, Ning users agree to use .ning as one of the extensions in their website. To create a Ning Network, go to www.ning.com, name your network and address, and click the orange "Create" button.

Next, fill in the information requested in the boxes provided.

When you are finished, click the orange "Sign Up" button near the bottom of the page.

Then, verify your Ning registration by accessing the email account you provided, and opening the email from Ning. Click on the link from Ning that will route you back to its website.

Now is your opportunity to describe your Ning Network. You can also decide if you want your network to be viewed by anyone or only people you invite to join and see it.

Further down the page, you can include keywords, plus set the website's language and country. After doing so, click the orange "Next" button near the bottom of the page.

Now you can add features and determine your website's layout. (Or, you could "Launch" your network and be online immediately.) If you're not quite ready to "launch", click on the orange "Next" button.

After clicking the "Next" button, choose a template.

Then, select from the themes and options provided to further personalize your network.

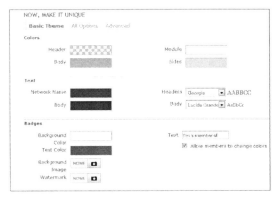

When you are finished, click on the orange "Launch" button at the bottom of the page. You are now online!

TWITTER: Twitter allows users to send and follow tweets. Tweets are text-only messages limited to 140 characters that are sent to the typist's account. Other registered Twitter users who follow the typist receive the tweet(s) by freely subscribing to the typist's feed. Several third parties have been granted limited access to Twitter in order to connect user-friendly applications that expand the reach of the program to other mediums like software programs and handheld devices.

Because of its intentional simplicity, Twitter can be used on cell phones, websites, voice mail systems, and email servers. Twitter is ideal for checking someone's status, organizing impromptu meetings, or sharing information instantaneously when other forms of communication are not convenient, or possible. For example, during the Iranian government's crackdowns on democracy protesters in 2009, many of the protesters sent real-time updates about the attacks after the government blocked traditional media and communications sources.

http://twitter.com/

http://computer.howstuffworks.com/internet/social-networking/networks/twitter.htm

From the Twitter homepage, click on the light green button "Sign up now" on the right.

Next, fill in the information requested in the boxes provided.

You will then be prompted to provide your email password so Twitter can see if contacts from your email address book are also tweeting. If you don't want to share your password, click "skip this step" under the button "Continue" at the bottom of the page.

The following page shows popular and celebrity Twitter users that you can follow. If not, click "skip this step" under the button "Finish" at the bottom of the page.

Finally, you will need to access the email account you provided when signing up to confirm your Twitter registration. Open the email from Twitter and click on the link directing you to confirm your registration. It will take you back to your main profile page where you can start tweeting and/or following those who do. Tweet and prosper!

MEETUP: Meetup allows users to connect with like-minded people for person-to-person meetings. The premise behind Meetup is that people organizing themselves locally can have a profound impact on their community, even the world. Once registered, the free

service allows members to search for groups and individuals sharing their interests. In the alternative, members can start a new group; say, to meet fellow patriot activists in their local community.

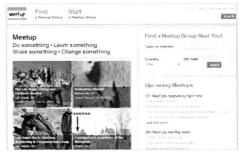

http://www.meetup.com/

Click on the words "Sign up" near the top right corner on the homepage.

Then, type in the information requested in the boxes provided. Click the button "Submit" when you are done.

You then must access the email address you gave in order to confirm your registration with Meetup. Open the email from Meetup and click on the link directing you to confirm your account.

After you confirm your account, the link will take you back to your Meetup profile page.

A little further down the page, you can input information on how far you would be willing to travel to meet other members, why you are joining Meetup, and upload a photo of yourself. When you're done, click "Submit" at the bottom of the page.

Chapter 10

Print

Even though newspapers are decreasing in circulation as readers go online for their news, the stories and opinions published by newspapers remain the primary source of delivering information. Nearly every newspaper maintains a website with as much, and often times more, information as their print version. Your goal is to get your group in their pages; digital if possible.

The best way is to submit an opinion column. Most news outlets crave content, don't want to pay for it, and prefer contributions from people within their readership. For instance, if you live in a suburban community covered by a local newspaper, you are far more likely to get a column published with it if you live in the community. Being able to claim yours is a "local perspective" is the most important pitch you can make to an editor. And all the better if you use title like, "Founder of the Springfield Tea Party."

So, if you held an event like a protest, Constitution seminar, or a funny demonstration, contact the paper or website you want to publish in and ask for their submission guidelines. (E.g. word count, deadlines, exclusivity, etc.) Once you've been published a few times, you'll have what the industry calls "clips," copies of your articles that you can send to larger, more influential papers and websites when you want to expand your reach.

The goal should be to get as much free publicity for your group as possible to attract as many like-minded people to the group as possible. As always, state a clear opinion, support it with sound arguments, and – when possible – use a bit of humor. People tend to repeat things that make them smile.

EasyMediaLists.com is the best single source for identifying personal contact information for print journalists and editors. For example, for less than $100 per list, several lists of the Top 100 US newspapers' editors can be accessed.

http://www.easymedialist.com/usa/top100newspapers.html

*The website's home page offers even more options, including USA national news media contacts, Spanish language news media contacts, and customized media lists.

http://www.easymedialist.com/   Easy Media List™

Chapter 11

Promotional Handout Items

People like free stuff, so long as it's helpful, funny, or small. Below are several online businesses to help you get started on campaign-type signs, bumper stickers, leaflets, banners, t-shirts, and the like. These kinds of materials are useful when you are trying to get attention from outsiders about something your group is doing or supporting. They help build awareness through advertising.

There are also more subtle ways to publicize your beliefs. After the 9/11 terrorist attacks many politicians learned the power of wearing small American flag lapel pin on their suit jackets. Almost nobody speaks directly about the pin, but everyone notices it. The same is true for the ever-present colored silicone wrist bands first popularized by champion cyclist Lance Armstrong. His were yellow like the lead jersey in the Tour de France, and said "Live Strong." Now, there are thousands of colors and messages being worn by millions of people. Like a semi-secret handshake, both of these items signal membership in an understated, attractive way.

Any of these items can get your group noticed, and make your members feel like they're a part of something professional and fun.

Brochures, Cards, Flyers and Handbill: There is a wealth of campaign-related websites able to fill just about any order for signs, brochures, banners, push-cards, flyers, buttons, and handbills. Among these are:

http://www.signelect.com/

http://www.runandwin.com

http://www.campaignbiz.com/

http://www.campaignheadquarters.com/materials.html

Apparel: CafePress.com is a company that allows individuals to design and order text and images imprinted on clothing and other apparel such as water bottles and buttons. There is no fixed number of items that must be ordered. Instead, CafePress uses on-demand printing to allow users to make and buy as many (or as few) customized products as they like. Another on-demand printing company is Zazzle.com.

http://www.cafepress.com/

http://www.zazzle.com/

http://www.thoseshirts.com/

http://www.thepeoplescube.com

Of all the internet websites dedicated to political commentary, *ThePeoplesCube.com* provides what may be the best example of telling the awful truth about Progressives coupled with a heavy dose of humor. The name of the website comes from a redesigned, fully licensed red Rubik's cube that guarantees "No More Competition!" and "Guaranteed Equality of Results!" Rush Limbaugh calls this website "The Stalinist version of The Onion" – a reference to both sites' biting sense of satire. *ThePeoplesCube. com* provides a wealth of commentary and products that will help drive home the silliness behind Progressive ideology. Be sure to check it out today!

Chapter 12

Create a Political Action Committee (PAC)

Money talks in politics. This is good because as a patriot activist you want politicians to listen. Now you know what ultimately gets their attention. So if you want to ensure that elected officials or those running to replace them hear your voice, you should seriously consider starting your own political action committee, or PAC.

Ordinarily, PACs are formed by businesses, labor organizations, ideological groups, or politicians. If the PAC is affiliated with an organization it is considered "connected" under federal elections law and must be registered with the Federal Elections Commission (FEC) within 10 days of forming. If the PAC is independent, it is "unconnected" and need only register when it distributes $1,000 in a calendar year to federal elections.

Contribution limitations do apply. PACs are limited to contributing $5,000 per election (primary, general, or special) to a candidate committee; $15,000 per year to a national party committee; and $5,000 per year to another PAC. The key to running a successful PAC is the ability to fundraise on behalf of your PAC's purpose. That way you can contribute to several campaigns, thus influencing several politicians.

Before you get started, make sure your desired PAC name is available. The FEC provides a comprehensive list of all the registered "PAC-ronyms" at the following website: *http://www.fec.gov/pubrec/pacronyms/ pacronyms.shtml*

When you decide on a name that isn't already registered, you're ready to start a PAC. After filing your paperwork with the FEC and maintaining accurate records for reporting purposes, you'll need to design a campaign strategy – not for you, but for your PAC. Since the whole point of creating a PAC is to raise and contribute money, you're now in the fundraising business!

Everything from the PAC's name to its motto, logo, and political purpose should be focused on creating an instantly recognizable brand. As the PAC's founder, you are selling at least two things. First, you're selling contributors on your ideas about "refounding" America. Then, you're selling candidates on the idea of accepting your contributors' money. The first sale is much harder than the second.

There are plenty of resources available online to hone your sales skills, but some tips are so universal they apply to any fundraising effort. First, make out a one page list of priorities with deadlines and budgets for each. Next, identify the group members that will help you run the PAC and delegate responsibilities according to each person's interest and ability. Then, create a presentation that is exciting to give, fun to hear, and chock full of memorable facts. For example, explain why you're targeting a specific city council race or a congressional primary. Tell your audience that candidates prefer contributions from inside their district because it lets them claim local support. Lastly, identify friendly groups in your community to present your sales pitch, and share your passion!

By the way, if you register as "non-connected," you'll want to read through a document from the FEC for "Nonconnected Committees," available at: *http://www.fec.gov/pdf/nongui.pdf* *

***Disclaimer:** This pdf was published in May 2008, and changes in campaign finance law are likely after the United States Supreme Court's decision in Citizens United v. FEC. As with creating any type of legal entity with tax consequences, you should consult the relevant expert to make sure you are in compliance with the applicable laws.

PART V: THE RESOURCES

"The inherent vice of capitalism is the unequal sharing of the blessings. The inherent blessing of socialism is the equal sharing of the misery."
-Winston Churchill

Here is where we connect you to the ideas, people, and institutions from across the political spectrum that are shaping our world.

You are not alone! The latest polls show that 41% of Americans hold conservative ideals. The number is rapidly rising. Currently, 35% of Americans now call themselves moderates, and only 21% identify as liberals or progressives. Their numbers are sharply down from over 33% in early-2009, as many people have become disillusioned by the big-government direction of the Obama Administration and the run-away spending of the Democrat-dominated Congress.

So why do we feel so isolated? Because most members of the "Main Stream Media" are progressives. They may be in the minority, but they hog the limelight.

Other patriots think and feel the way that we do, and most of them are accessible on the Internet.

In the following pages you will find links and descriptions of the websites, blogs, media outlets, books, and think tanks that will help you expand your knowledge base of friend and foe alike. Dig in!

Chapter 1 provides a list of the top-26 classic conservative books to read, and then the best current books dealing with political issues in the post 9/11 era.

Chapter 2 gives a list of the top patriot activist websites that cover a variety of missions including organization, education, and social network.

Chapter 3 lists the top conservative & libertarian websites.

Chapter 4 lists the prominent conservative and libertarian organizations.

Chapter 5 gives information about conservative and libertarian litigations groups that defend the rights of individuals against government encroachment. These firms will take on important issues at their own expense.

Chapter 6 shows our "Top-10" most popular "mainstream media" (MSM) websites including network and cable news, and nationally circulated weekly magazines. All are edited by progressives - except one. Guess who...?

Chapter 7 includes a list of the most popular progressive activist websites.

Chapter 8 lists prominent progressive/socialist/Marxist/statist "think tanks".

Bear in mind that what follows is just the tip of the iceberg! The primary goal of this Resources section is to connect you with our private website which is loaded with lots more ideas, strategies, and supports that you can load into your own personal arsenal of "weapons of truth". There is much more information to tap into.

 Go to *www.RefoundingAmericaBook.com* and log in right now. It's free! And it's available only to you!

On the bottom left-hand side of the last page of this book is a unique serial number. It looks something like this: 123456XX00001A/1/P. Simply enter it into the "For Insiders Only" box on our website: *www.RefoundingAmericaBook.com*. You will then be able to create your own unique ID & password to access the private closed sections.

Here's one feature: all of the organizations and web sites listed in the following chapters are also on our web site - with hyperlinks that you can click on to take you immediately to their own home pages.

And there's much more. Want to reach a specific Congressman & Senator, or Governor & State Legislator? All their fax numbers, phone numbers, e-mail addresses and physical addresses are provided for your personal use!

Want to reach your local newspaper or news director of your TV stations? Their contact information is included as well.

Chapter 1

Top Books to Read On Freedom

A patriot activist cannot live on the Internet alone. We need information that helps us go deeper into issues and ideas so that we don't just consume information; we grow from it. Thus, we need books. Fortunately, we have a rich heritage of freedom-loving thinkers to look to.

This chapter divides the important books to read into two categories:

First Principles, and *Post 9/11 Books*

The first section lists twenty-six books covering the importance of freedom and the need to recognize the universal ongoing failures of the progressives/socialists/Marxists/statists. The ideas animating much of public policy and political philosophy today did battle during the 20th century and before. The truth has not changed. Some of these books were written over one hundred years ago. Some were written in 2009. They all speak to how individual freedom has been defended and persevered in the recent past against the ravages of communism and fascism.

Since the Islamist terrorist attack of 9/11, a number of books have been published arguing for renewed adherence to traditional American notions about freedom. Sadly, in our post-9/11 nation, there are many politicians in Washington who seek to disregard the lessons of the recent past by sacrificing our personal liberties for perceived security provided by the State. Big Brother and the Nanny State have been growing unchecked under both the previous Republican and the current Democratic administrations.

In its own way, each book in the post-9/11 section points out the fallacies of progressive thinking and applies the logic of freedom to our current problems. In sum, the books in both sections provide an opportunity to read and reflect upon the consequences of ideas.

First Principles: Twenty-six Books You Should Read
(see: *www.LeadershipInstitute.org*)

Robert Bartley, *The Seven Fat Years*
This book provides an explanation and defense of the "Reaganomics" revolution from 1982-87 that spurred unprecedented economic growth through supply-side economics.

Frederic Bastiat, *The Law*
This book is a classic text defining law as an organized system of self-defense designed to protect life, liberty, and property.

William F. Buckley, Jr., *Up from Liberalism*
This book at once gives an excellent history lesson on 1960s-era progressivism with a combination of humor and erudition that is timeless.

Peter Stanlis, *Selected Writings and Speeches of Edmund Burke collected*
In many ways, Edmund Burke is the intellectual father of modern conservatism, especially the notion of ordered liberty. This book selects some of his best work for serious study.

James Burnham, *Suicide of the West*
This book shows how progressivism is the preliminary stage that allows communism to take hold.

Whitaker Chambers, *Witness*
This book is an autobiographical account of the author's one-time association with the Communist Party of the United States, and his decision to testify against Communists inside the federal government.

Dinesh D'Souza, *Ronald Reagan*
This book makes the case for Ronald Reagan being one of the greatest presidents in American history due to the economic growth and collapse of Soviet power during and after his presidency.

Allen Drury, *Advise and Consent*
This book is a classic political novel written by a veteran Washington political reporter and ardent anti-communist.

M. Stanton Evans, *The Theme Is Freedom*
This book is a path-breaking refutation of Marxist atheism. Contra Marx, the author demonstrates that a country's freedom comes from its religious principles.

F.A. Hayek, *The Road to Serfdom*
This book is a highly readable explanation of why socialism cannot work.

F.A. Hayek, *The Fatal Conceit*
This book shows that the chief error of socialism is its belief that man can

remake the world according to his wishes.

Milton Friedman, *Capitalism and Freedom*
This book is a jargon-free argument for economic freedom being a precondition for political freedom.

Barry Goldwater, *Conscience of a Conservative*
This book is credited by many as the spark that ignited the grassroots conservative movement that eventually propelled Ronald Reagan to the presidency.

Henry Hazlitt, *Economics in One Lesson*
This book is universally acclaimed as the best (and one of the shortest) introductions to basic economic theory in print.

Douglas Hyde, *Dedication and Leadership*
This book is the autographical work of a former British Communist Party official who converted to Christianity. It explains the philosophically neutral communication techniques used by communists to attract people and legitimacy.

Paul Johnson, *Modern Times*
This book is a highly readable history of the twentieth century from the 1920s to the 1990s unburdened by a progressive perspective.

Russell Kirk, *The Conservative Mind*
Along with the more popularized works of William F. Buckley, Jr., this book by Russell Kirk re-established the intellectual credibility of conservative principles in America during the 1950s.

Mark Levin, *Liberty and Tyranny*
A 2009 bestseller, this book is one of the best recent encapsulations of the American political conservative philosophy.

Eugene Methvin, *The Rise of Radicalism*
This book examines the strategies and tactics that modern Leftist organizations use to intimidate opposition while capturing public opinion.

Frank Meyer, *Defense of Freedom*
This book lays the intellectual groundwork for fusing free-market and social-issue conservatives into a mutually enhancing movement capable of winning elections.

Frank Meyer, *What Is Conservatism?*
Another book by the conservative fusionist Frank Meyer, this installment continues the argument that economic and social conservatives are far more similar than different.

Ayn Rand, *Atlas Shrugged*
This book is a classic essay-turned-novel indictment of the evils of socialism.

William Riordon, *Plunkitt of Tammany Hall*
This book is an excellent analysis of big-city politics as practiced by machine politicians.

Thomas Sowell, *Knowledge and Decisions*
This book is a penetrating study on the limits of bureaucratic knowledge and decision making.

Richard Viguerie, *The New Right: We're Ready To Lead*
This book is an excellent piece of history for budding conservative activists to read because it details the rise of the Reagan coalition of Republicans, Independents & Democrats in the 1970s.

Richard Weaver, *Ideas Have Consequences*
This book is short but deep in its remedy for what ails modern man: regaining faith, and promoting good ideas through skillful actions.

Post 9/11 Books on Personal Freedom versus The State

Glenn Beck, *Arguing with Idiots: How to Stop Small Minds and Big Government (2009)*
This book is a humorous, fact-filled response to the most common progressive/socialist public policy arguments. Must read.

Mark Levin, *Liberty and Tyranny: A Conservative Manifesto (2009)*
A 2009 bestseller, this book is one of the best recent encapsulations of the American political conservative philosophy.

Sean Hannity, *Deliver Us from Evil: Defeating Terrorism, Despotism, and Progressivism (2004)*
This book voices full-throated support for former President George W. Bush's policy of pre-emptive war against terror-sponsoring nations. It also critiques the progressive tendency to dialogue with – rather than defeat – America's enemies.

Laura Ingraham, *Power to the People (2007)*
This book argues for conservatives to take back the phrase "power to the people" from the radical left, and apply it to the majority of Americans who believe in traditional values.

Dick Morris, *Catastrophe: How Obama, Congress, and the Special Interests are Transforming...A Slump into a Crash, Freedom into Socialism, and a Disaster into a Catastrophe...And How to Fight Back (2009)*
This book is an indictment of the Obama presidency and its tendencies towards socialism in every area of American life.

Michelle Malkin, *Culture of Corruption: Obama and His Team of Tax Cheats, Crooks, and Cronies (2009)*

Jim DeMint, *Saving Freedom: We Can Stop America's Slide into Socialism (2009)*
This book is a mix of warnings against socialism and proposals to fix the problems that lead many people to support socialist policies.

Jonah Goldberg, *Progressive Fascism: The Secret History of the American Left, From Mussolini to the Politics of Meaning (2007)*
This book is a provocative examination of the Progressive's fascination with fascism, including parallels between Nazi Germany and the New Deal.

Ann Coulter, *Guilty: Progressive "Victims" and Their Assault on America (2009)*
In this book Ann Coulter explains how Progressives use the language of victimhood to mask their oppressive policies on those outside the chosen class of victims.

All these great books are available for immediate order on our book website. And many of the resources and books mentioned in *Refounding America* are available for free PDF download just for you. Also, you'll find a helpful list of pro-freedom movies worth watching on our website. Go to *www.RefoundingAmericaBook.com* and log in to our Insiders section.

Chapter 2

Top Patriot Activist Web Sites

There comes a point in every political discussion when the participants must move from talk to action. Cyberspace is filled with fellow patriot activists who are organizing, educating, and mobilizing others to *Refound America*. The websites in this chapter range from social networking groups to political action committees (PACs). We've also included organizations that train activists to support individual freedoms and fight against the progressive/socialist/Marxist/corporate takeover of Washington.

These are the most important peer groups for people looking to put thoughts into action because they are engaged in planning rallies, raising money, contacting elected officials, and winning campaigns. In short, this chapter will plug you into the Classical Liberal, Conservative & Libertarian patriot grassroots. Take their ideas and use them in your local community.

9-12 MOMS
www.9-12moms.ning.com
Also known as *Conservative Moms for America*, this group provides a forum to meet and converse with mothers working to create a better American future for their children.

THE 912 PROJECT
www.the912project.com
Founded and supported by Glenn Beck, this group is organized around his 9 principles and 12 values. In 2010, the group is promoting Mr. Beck's "The Plan" to reorient America towards becoming a republic of freedom. Check this site out first!

THE AMERICAN CONSERVATIVE UNION
www.conservative.org
ACU is the nation's oldest and largest grassroots conservative lobbying organization. They provide instant communications links between citizens

and politicians. *ACU* also rates federal legislators that are the gold standard for determining a congressman's level of commitment to individual liberty - and against Big Brother statism.

AMERICANS FOR PROSPERITY

www.americansforprosperity.org
AFP educates citizens about economics and assists them in influencing the public policy process at the state and national levels.

AMERICANS FOR TAX REFORM

www.atr.org
ATR opposes any increases in personal or business income tax rates. Period. To promote this, *ATR* encourages state and federal office seekers to sign the group's "Taxpayer Protection Pledge."

AMERICAN LIBERTY ALLIANCE

www.americanlibertyalliance.com
American Liberty Alliance is an umbrella organization for a network of grassroots activists dedicated to securing greater economic and individual freedom. A major Tea-Party organizer.

AS A MOM

www.asamom.ning.com
Describing itself as "A Sisterhood of Mommy Patriots", *As A Mom* is a website offering mothers inspired by the 9-12 Project's 9 principles and 12 values way to coordinate and meet other mothers. Started by a Glenn Beck viewer, *As A Mom* is active in the ongoing national We The People marches and demonstrations.

AYN RAND CENTER FOR INDIVIDUAL RIGHTS

www.aynrand.org
A project of the Irvine, CA-based Ayn Rand Institute, *ARC* promotes public policy applications of Rand's Objectivist philosophy to economic and foreign policy issues.

BUREAU CRASH (The Freedom Activist Network)
www.bureaucrash.com
An online meet-up and resource forum, *Bureau Crash* enables a network of activists (called "crashers") to use guerilla marketing and new media to influence people and policies towards free-market and individual liberty thinking. Check this site out, especially for their Capitalism teashirts.

CAMPAIGN FOR LIBERTY
www.campaignforliberty.com
Founded by Congressman Ron Paul, this group champions traditional libertarian principles in economic and foreign affairs, including Ron Paul's "Audit the Fed" bill. Another great resource is Paul's website *www.FREE-NEFL.com.*

CENTER FOR INDIVIDUAL FREEDOM
www.cfif.org
CFIF seeks to promote and protect individual rights and freedoms through commentary, litigation, and educational outreach.

CITIZENS AGAINST GOVERNMENT WASTE
www.cagw.org
CAGW researches, identifies, and publicizes instances of government waste in spending, management, and inefficiency. A goldmine of corruption exposed. Oink. Oink.

THE CLUB FOR GROWTH
www.clubforgrowth.org
Founded by Steven Moore, now with the Wall Street Journal, *CFG* encourages policies that stimulate economic growth through expanding the free market and endorses viable political candidates that support these ideas through its active PAC.

FREE REPUBLIC
www.freerepublic.com
A popular news & blog site, *Free Republic* aggregates the latest antics of the Progressives from the newswire stories.

FREEDOM WORKS
www.freedomworks.org
Freedom Works is a Washington, D.C.-based classical liberal activist network that educates, coordinates, and mobilizes small government patriots around the country.

GIVE ME LIBERTY
www.givemeliberty.org
One of the principal organizers of the "Continental Congress 2009" in St. Charles, IL, *Give Me Liberty* created the "We the People Foundation" and the "Jekyll Island Project". Check this out.

GRASSFIRE
www.grassfire.com
Grassfire provides conservative activists with resources for coordinating rallies and communications, including on-line links for sending instant e-mails to Congress.

GUN OWNERS OF AMERICA
www.gunowners.org
Ron Paul calls *GOA*: "The only no-compromise gun lobby in Washington." Enough said.

HOWARD JARVIS TAXPAYERS ASSOCIATION
www.hjta.org
Founded in 1978 to protest the rise in California's property taxes, *HJTA* was responsible for passing California's Proposition 13, a state constitutional amendment that capped runaway property tax increases. It continues to support property tax caps and other tax reduction policies.

INSTITUTE FOR LIBERTY
www.instituteforliberty.org
IFL is an aggressive advocate for small business interests in the federal legislative and regulatory process. It covers issues important to every lover of liberty. Check this out.

LEADERSHIP INSTITUTE
www.leadershipinstitute.org
Founded by Morton Blackwell, the *Leadership Institute* is one of the most important organizations supporting the Classical Liberal. *LI* focuses on training patriot activists in how to organize campaigns, projects, and outreach efforts in order to win arguments and majorities. They run training seminars nationwide. Check this out - and enroll in their local programs!

LET FREEDOM RING
www.letfreedomringusa.com
Created with the purpose to recruit, educate, motivate, and support conservative activists, this organization seeks to counter progressive attacks on constitutional government, economic freedom, and traditional values.

LIBERTY OR DEATH
www.patrickhenrycenter.com
A supporter of the Tea Party movement, the *Patrick Henry Center* has a special interest in assisting whistleblowers. If you have insider information on corrupt politicians or government agencies, here's the place to share your story.

MIL MOMS
www.militarymomsofamerica.ning.com
Mil(itary) Moms is a support and educational website for mothers of military personnel who strongly support our American troops who are risking their lives on the frontlines to defend our freedoms everyday. They also provides information on legislation and issues pertinent to military families.

M.O.M. 4 AMERICA
www.mom4america.ning.com
Millions of Moms (M.O.M.) for America is the national website for mothers looking to connect with others about how to educate and organize for a better America. The site also provides links to state and affinity group chapters.

THE NATIONAL 912 COALITION

www.thenational912coalition.net
The National 912 Coalition seeks to help affiliated individuals and groups organize for joint action around the 9 principles and 12 values of the 9-12 Project.

NATIONAL RIFLE ASSOCIATION
www.NRA.org
Founded by Union veterans Col. William C. Church and Gen. George Wingate in 1871, the *NRA* is the principle organization which actively supports the 2nd Amendment right for the individual law-abiding citizen to own and bear arms. It actively works with other organizations to defend the Bill of Rights of Americans against the government. Join it today!

NATIONAL TAX-LIMITATION COMMITTEE PAC

www.limittaxes.com
NTLC exists to reduce the overall tax burden at every level of government in order to give individuals and businesses more room to grow.

NATIONAL TAXPAYERS UNION

www.ntu.org
NTU advocates lower taxes and measures such as federal amendment limiting tax increases and requiring Congress to pass a balanced budget. The granddaddy of the taxpayers movement.

OUR COUNTRY DESERVES BETTER PAC

www.ourcountrydeservesbetter.com
This group links visitors to a number of campaigns that fellow activists can contribute time and money to, such as the "*Tea Party Express.*"   One of the major patriot activist PACS.

RESIST NET

www.resistnet.com
The official social network of *Grassfire Nation*, *ResistNet* seeks to give those upset about the progressive direction of America a place to voice their opinions with like-minded people.

RIGHT MARCH
www.rightmarch.com
Right March helps to counter the Statist's and Marxist's demonstrations and communications by empowering conservative activists to organize rapid response strategies.

SENATE CONSERVATIVES FUND
www.senateconservatives.com
SCF is an independent Political Action Committee dedicated to electing conservatives - Republicans, Independents & Democrats - to the United States Senate. It is NOT an organ of the Republican Party.

TAX DAY TEA PARTY
www.taxdayteaparty.com
This group provides patriot activists with support for meeting and organizing fellow peaceful tax protesters. Big events on April 15 happen in Washington and at Federal Buildings throughout the country. One of the major grassroots organizers.

TEA PARTY
www.teaparty.org
Founded by former Marine Dale Robertson, *TeaParty* is one of the first Tea Party movement websites for activists, and a resource for connecting to other similar groups. Check it out.

TEA PARTY EXPRESS
www.teapartyexpress.org
TeaPartyExpress is one of the patriot movement's founders. This is the website for information about the ubiquitous bus tours that rally support and local media coverage for Tea Party gatherings nationwide as the wind their way to Washington, DC. Check this site out. Important.

TEA PARTY NATION
www.teapartynation.com
TPN is one of the most influential groups in the Tea Party Movement be-

cause of its leadership in organizing a national convention and providing a forum for patriot activists to "quench their thirst for freedom!"

TEA PARTY PATRIOTS
www.teapartypatriots.org
Tea Party Patriots is one of the original organizations of classical liberal patriots, with over 50,000 nationwide members. Blogs, articles & strategies Tea Party movement members. Their new project *ContractFromAmerica. com* presents specific ideas to fix broken government at both the national and state levels. Check this site out.

WE THE PEOPLE REVOLUTION
www.wethepeoplerevolution.com
We the People Revolution provides an excellent on-line "crash course" (2.5 hours) in getting up to speed on traditional American philosophy and the mechanics of government. The provide specific game plans for effectively engaging elected officials and the media, and planning events with and for fellow activists. Check out their free Next Step presentation. Must view site.

YOUNG AMERICANS FOR LIBERTY
www.yaliberty.org
An extension of Students for Ron Paul, YAL recruits, trains, educates, and mobilizes students -both college and high school - on the ideals of liberty and the Constitution.

YOUNG AMERICA'S FOUNDATION
www.yaf.org
YAF introduces high school and college age students to the ideas of the American Founding, including individual freedom, a strong national defense, free enterprise, and traditional values through local campus chapters and famous national speakers. *YAF* also operates the *Ronald Reagan Center, Ronald Reagan Ranch*, and the *National Journalism Center.*

Chapter 3

Top Conservative & Libertarian Web Sites

If your head is about to explode from overexposure to the Main Stream Media's distortions and lies, this chapter offers a chance to regain perspective. Remember that most people get their news today on the Internet, and there are plenty of great news sources from the classical liberal perspective.

Here you will find everything from news "aggregators" to original reporting and commentary. You will also find social networking sites and resources to identify and combat progressive media bias. Here are the best of the best, ranked.

TOP NEWS & INFORMATION SOURCES

No. 1: DRUDGE REPORT
www.drudgereport.com
A news aggregation website with a conservative perspective on US politics, *The Drudge Report* became a national news source when its founder, Matt Drudge, broke the Monica Lewinsky story. Drudge usually hears about it first. Great source of real news from UK-newspapers.

No. 2: NEWSMAX
www.newsmax.com
The online version of the monthly print publication by the same name, *Newsmax* provides news and opinion commentary from a conservative perspective. A print edition is also on newsstands.

No. 3: WORLD NET DAILY
www.wnd.com
WND creates content from conservative and libertarian viewpoints, links to commentary from other websites, and publishes books under the imprint *WND Books*.

No. 4: BREITBART.com
www.breitbart.com
A news website with substantial ties between its founder, Andrew Breitbart, and The Drudge Report, *Breitbart.com* also provides links to special-
ized interest blogs and original news material at sister sites *BigGovernment.
com*, *BigHollywood.com*, and *BigJournalism.com*. Must read.

TOP THREE MEDIA PERSONALITIES

No. 1: RUSH LIMBAGUH
www.rushlimbaugh.com
Rush Limbaugh is the most listened to radio commentator in America
reaching millions of listeners via 600 stations. His opinions matter – just
ask the Obama Administration.

No. 2: SEAN HANNITY
www.hannity.com
Sean Hannity is one of the most ubiquitous conservative media personalities in American with nationwide followings in radio and on television.

OTHER IMPORTANT WEBSITES

THE AMERICAN CONSERVATIVE
www.amconmag.com
The American Conservative is the premier classical liberal print and online
publication in America, advocating a restrained foreign policy and federal
government. Also on newsstands.

AMERICAN THINKER
www.americanthinker.com
The American Thinker is a conservative website featuring original content
on issues in American culture, the economy, and foreign policy. A print
version is on newsstands.

COMMENTARY MAGAZINE
www.commentarymagazine.com

Founded at the end of WWII, *Commentary Magazine* is a leading neo-conservative voice on national defense and maintaining high culture in an era of political correctness.

DISCOVER THE NETWORKS
www.discoverthenetworks.org

A project of the David Horowitz Freedom Center, *Discover the Networks* is an innovative resource for finding and connecting progressive individuals, groups, funders, media, issues, politics, academia, and arts & culture.

FRONT PAGE MAGAZINE
www.frontpagemag.com

Founded by former left-wing radical David Horowitz, *Front Page Magazine* critiques left-wing radicalism and the progressive bias in higher education

HOT AIR
www.hotair.com

The "other" blog founded and hosted by Michelle Malkin. *Hot Air* specializes in not only written content, but also in creating original videos and features. One of today's leading thinkers.

HUMAN EVENTS
www.humanevents.com

One of the oldest conservative publications, *Human Events* was founded in 1944 and takes its name from the first line of the Declaration of Independence: "When in the course of human events…" It publishes commentary by major conservative writers. Located on Capitol Hill.

INFO WARS
www.infowars.com

This website is administered by talk radio host Alex Jones for those who want an informational alternative to biased liberal news. Sections cover:

the Economic Crisis, September 11, the Constitution, Illegal immigration, the Police State, and the Media.

INSTAPUNDIT
www.pajamasmedia.com/instapundit
Created by University of Tennessee law professor Glenn Reynolds, *Insta-Pundit* was launched in 2001 as a class experiment teaching Internet law. It has since become one of the most-read political blogs in America. Also see the main web site *Pajamasmedia*.com for lots more political news and pundit blogs from some of the brightest classical liberal minds.

JUDICIAL WATCH
www.judicialwatch.org
Judicial Watch is a government watchdog that emphasizes integrity and ethical behavior from elected and appointed officials "because no one is above the law". JW uses the Freedom of Information Act to pry loose data on corruption documented by the trail of government e-mails.

MICHELLE MALKIN
www.michellemalkin.com
Founder and primary contributor *Michelle Malkin* has made her eponymous blog one of the heaviest trafficked blogs of any type on the Internet. The blog is written from a conservative perspective.

NATIONAL REVIEW ONLINE
www.nationalreview.com
Founded by William F. Buckley, who almost single-handedly re-created classical liberalism in the 1960's with the *National Review* magazine (on newsstands). *NRO*, posts new content and links to other blogs and websites daily. Its primary blog, corner.nationalreview.com, is one of the most read conservative blogs - with commentators on both the Left and the Right.

NEWSBUSTERS
www.newsbusters.org
Newsbusters is a blog project of the Media Research Center (MRC), a conservative watchdog group dedicated to exposing progressive media bias.

POLITICO
www.politico.com

Though it's the place to get full-spectrum news and views of "inside Washington" many progressives consider it a "conservative" outlet. That's the price for even-handed reporting.

POWERLINE
www.powerlineblog.com

Powerline is a political commentary blog run by conservative attorneys. Good legal analysis.

REASON MAGAZINE
www.reason.com

The granddaddy libertarian publication by the *Reason Foundation*, Reason Magazine provides a libertarian analysis and commentary on politics, policy, and culture. Also on newsstands.

RED STATE
www.redstate.com

Red State is the sister site of Human Events. It is one of the most popular political blogs of any persuasion and the most cited right of center blog by the media. Owned by Eagle Publishing, whose Regnery Books publishes best-selling Ann Coulter and the popular P.I.G. series of titles.

SOURCE WATCH
www.sourcewatch.org

This website is a collaborative, Wikipedia-style endeavor that provides information about "the names behind the news", including public relations firms, think tanks, and industry-funded organizations and experts. An excellent resource for getting the back story on spin doctors.

STOP THE ACLU
www.stoptheaclu.com

Resourced by independent writers, this website is dedicated to exposing the dangers to America posed by the *ACLU's* radical agenda. For the classical liberal's '*ACLU*', see: *www.ACLJ.org*.

TENTH AMENDMENT CENTER
www.tenthamendmentcenter.com

The Tenth Amendment Center advocates reinvigorating the Tenth Amendment to the US Constitution, especially its power to check Washington's overreach by protecting each of the 50 states' sovereignty.

TOWNHALL
www.townhall.com

Originally established by a conservative think tank, *The Heritage Foundation, Townhall* is both a daily online and monthly print publication now owned by Salem Communications. It primarily targets a conservative audience with news and commentary provided by conservative journalists, politicians, and strategists.

THE WEEKLY STANDARD
www.weeklystandard.com

The Weekly Standard is the premier neoconservative publication in America, advocating an activist foreign policy and federal government. A print edition is also on newsstands.

Chapter 4

Top Conservative & Libertarian Think Tanks

Think tanks that support the individual and our personal freedoms come in all shapes and sizes. They support the broad values of the classical liberal views of the Founding Fathers: protection of the citizen from the State, limited government with strong checks & balances over its power, and a free-market system. They generally reflect two basic political strains: conservative and libertarian. Many have associated PAC's which lobby for their interests.

The similarities between the two are striking. In fact, the fusion of libertarian and conservative ideas about government did much to propel the Republican Party into power in the 1980s and 1990s. Both recognize the fundamental importance of individual freedom to enable human flourishing. Both advocate for limited government in the free market and civil society. Their differences usually arise in how much to limit the government's regulatory role in particular issues and to its overseas military presence in 100+ countries.

Libertarians are often perceived as a bit too anarchistic for the conservative sensibility. Conservatives are sometimes perceived as a bit too soft on government for the libertarian spirit. Today, the libertarian part of the Republican Party, as represented by Representative Ron Paul and Senate candidate Peter Schiff, is rapidly growing in strength, assisted by Internet-based fund-raising drives.

Though there are differences of opinion throughout the conservative-libertarian spectrum, our ongoing discussion enables a robust exploration and extension of first principles that tests and strengthens our strong friendship and common belief in the rights of the individual versus the state's power to rule over him. When compared against the progressive/socialist/Marxist/statist position of all-encompassing big government, the differences dissolve.

Interestingly, the recent absence of a counter-point within the progressive/socialist/ Marxist/statist think tank community is now driving away many of the very people who would support classical liberal ideas such as freedom of privacy, protection of the middle class worker, and support for the natural rights of women & non-Muslims in Muslim countries.

CONSERVATIVE ORGANIZATIONS:

ACTON INSTITUTE FOR THE STUDY OF
RELIGION AND LIBERTY

www.acton.org
Named after the English historian and moralist, Lord John Acton (1834-1902) who said: "Power tends to corrupt, and absolute power corrupts absolutely", *The Acton Institute* encourages a society that is both free and virtuous. It holds seminars and publishes various books, monographs, periodicals, and articles, including the *Journal of Markets & Morality.*

AMERICAN ENTERPRISE INSTITUTE
www.aei.org
 One of the oldest conservative think tanks in America, the *American Enterprise Institute* specializes in research and commentary on economic, defense, health, legal, and social policy. Publisher of The American magazine, on magazine stands nationwide.

AMERICAN ISRAEL PUBLIC AFFAIRS
COMMITTEE (AIPAC)
www.aipac.org
Part public affairs organization, part periodical publisher, *AIPAC* is the premier pro-Israel lobbying group and PAC in America.

CENTER FOR IMMIGRATION
STUDIES

www.cis.org
The *Center For Immigration Studies* describes itself as America's "only think tank devoted exclusively to research and policy analysis of the economic, social, demographic, fiscal, and other impacts of immigration on the United States." Legal versus illegal immigration issues.

CENTER FOR SECURITY
POLICY

www.centerforsecuritypolicy.org
Founded in 1988, *CSP* seeks to promote "peace through strength" by ana-

lyzing and implementing policies to ensure America's continued national security and global preeminence.

CLAREMONT INSTITUTE

The Claremont Institute
For the Study of Statesmanship and Political Philosophy

www.claremont.org

The Claremont Institute promotes the ideals of the American founding and aims to refocus citizens' and government's attention on recovering respect for the life, liberty, and property of individuals and families.

COMMITTEE ON THE PRESENT DANGER

The Committee on the Present Danger
fighting terrorism and the ideologies that drive it

www.committeeonthepresentdanger.org

CPD is primarily an advocacy organization pursuing a vigorous call to action to defeat Islamic terrorism and tyrannical aggression from both state and non-state actors.

FOREIGN POLICY RESEARCH INSTITUTE

FOREIGN POLICY RESEARCH INSTITUTE
Providing Ideas in Service to Our Nation Since 1955

www.fpri.org

FPRI is a conservative foreign policy think tank focusing on issues related to terrorism, the Middle East, nuclear proliferation, as well as relations with China, Russia, and Japan.

FOUNDATION FOR DEFENSE OF DEMOCRACIES

www.defenddemocracy.org

A top think-tank with emphasis on global jihad, and defense issues, *FDD* focuses exclusively on the ideologies and movements driving terrorism. Outstanding thinkers and prolific writers include fellows Walid Phares (*Fox News* contributor) and Claudia Rosett, former WSJ editor (*JohnBatchelorShow.com* contributor). Must read.

GOLDWATER INSTITUTE

GOLDWATER
INSTITUTE

www.goldwaterinstitute.org

This Phoenix, AZ based institute helps ensure constitutionally limited government through litigation. It also contributes research and commentary to promote individual liberty and personal responsibility.

HERITAGE FOUNDATION
www.heritage.org
The Heritage Foundation produces research and commentary promoting conservative public policies "based on the principles of free enterprise, limited government, individual freedom, traditional American values, and a strong national defense." Major publisher. Must view.

HOOVER INSTITUTION
www.hoover.org
Part of Stanford University, *The Hoover Institution* is a touchstone in conservative and libertarian circles, providing research and commentary supporting representative government, private enterprise, peace, personal freedom, and the safeguards of the American system.

HUDSON INSTITUTE
www.hudson.org
The Hudson Institute specializes in studying the "interplay among culture, demography, technology, markets, and political leadership."

MANHATTAN INSTITUTE
www.manhattan-institute.org
Located in New York City, the *Manhattan Institute* speaks on a broad set of issues including health care, counterterrorism, education, and urban renewal, among others. It has also helped craft reform legislation that has been implemented at the local, state, and national levels of government. One of the major classical liberal think tanks. Worth checking out.

NATIONAL CENTER FOR POLICY ANALYSIS
www.ncpa.org
Noted for contributions to promoting conservative health care reform policies, *NCPA* also supports free-market-based solutions to problems found in health care, taxes, Social Security, welfare, criminal justice, education, environmental regulation.

PACIFIC RESEARCH INSTITUTE
www.liberty.pacificresearch.org
San Francisco, CA based PRI provides research and commentary on education, business and economics, health care, technology, and the environment from a conservative, free-market perspective. A key member of the *State Policy Network (www.SPN.org).*

LIBERTARIAN & CLASSICAL LIBERAL THINK TANKS:

ATLAS ECONOMIC RESEARCH FOUNDATION
www.atlasnetwork.org
Atlas is not a think tank per se, but rather an organization that helps create and support free-market think tanks worldwide. A strong supporter of Austrian Economics, several Nobel Prize winners in Economics are associated with the institution. Great reference site on economics.

CATO INSTITUTE
www.cato.org
Based in Washington, D.C., *CATO* is the premier national libertarian think tank providing a well-respected platform for disseminating ideas "that create free, open, and civil societies in the United States and throughout the world." One of the top organizations in the world. Must read.

COMPETITIVE ENTERPRISE INSTITUTE
www.cei.org
CEI offers its free-market-based research and commentary on a wide range of issues, summing up its areas of interest as follows: "If the government has written rules to regulate it, we have an opinion on how it could be done better."

FOUNDATION FOR ECONOMIC EDUCATION
www.fee.org
Founded in 1946 by Leonard Read, *FEE* is the original source of all the classical liberal think tanks in the United States. *FEE* strongly promotes

the ideals of the American founding, including the rule of law, individual choice and liberty, and the free market. Download the classic I, Pencil from their website. Lots more.

FOUNDATION FOR RESEARCH ON
ECONOMICS AND THE ENVIRONMENT
www.free-eco.org
FREE-ECO's mission "is to work with opinion leaders and decision makers to demonstrate how science and economics can effectively deal with contentious policy issues in ways consistent with a society of free and responsible individuals and America's founding ideals."

HEARTLAND INSTITUTE
www.heartland.org
Based in Chicago, IL, the *Heartland Institute* is a nationally-focused institute creating research and commentary on state and national policy issues with a strong emphasis on promoting limited government and the free market. It also focuses on global warming, education & energy. Enormous amount of facts & figures including papers and Powerpoint's from hundreds of expert speakers at its three International Symposiums on Climate Change held in 2009. Must View.

INDEPENDENT INSTITUTE
www.independent.org
The Independent Institute provides research and commentary from a libertarian perspective on a wide range of issues. Major book publisher. Great "neutral" site for the Independent thinker.

LEXINGTON INSTITUTE
www.lexingtoninstitute.org
Based in Arlington, VA, the nationally-focused *Lexington Institute* "actively opposes the unnecessary intrusion of the federal government into the commerce and culture of the nation, and strives to find nongovernmental, market-based solutions to public policy challenges."

LUDWIG VON MISES INSTITUTE
www.mises.org
The Mises Institute is the "world center of the Austrian School of economics and libertarian political and social theory." Along with hosting a summer school for college students, it publishes books, newsletters, and commentary from Austrian economists like Mises, F.A. Hayek, Henry Hazlitt, Murray N. Rothbard and Lew Rockwell.

MERCATUS CENTER
www.mercatus.org
Based in Arlington, VA, the *Mercatus Center* is the free-market site of George Mason University, the nation's foremost Austrian Economics School. Walter Williams, the famous black American fill-in host for Rush Limbaugh is the Economics Chair Emeritus.

PROGRESS AND FREEDOM FOUNDATION
www.pff.org
PFF focuses on regulatory issues related to the "digital revolution" by producing research and commentary "about issues associated with technological change, based on a philosophy of limited government, free markets, and individual sovereignty."

REASON FOUNDATION
www.reason.org
Located in Los Angeles, CA, the *Reason Foundation* produces rigorously reviewed research and searching commentary on issues effecting local, state, and national policy makers, including Reason Magazine, on newsstands nationwide. Their Reason.tv project also offers a healthy dose of humor to counter statist madness.

Chapter 5

Top Conservative & Libertarian Litigation Groups

The groups in this chapter step forward to defend individuals when government lawmakers or agencies violate their rights. If you or someone you know is restricted from using personally-owned property, discriminated against on the basis of religion, or believes that a law violates the Constitution, then these are the public interest attorneys to turn to for help. Whether as full-timers or volunteers, these lawyers are the legal bulwark for protecting We The People from the abuses of an overzealous government.

They are often looking for nationwide volunteers who can help out with the on-going battle against an increasingly corrupt and corporate-leaning State. These patriotic attorneys may, in the end, be the last defense against the abuses of the clearly unconstitutional activities of a big-spending, big-tax, big-welfare, big-military centralized-control behemoth.

ALLIANCE DEFENSE FUND
www.alliancedefensefund.org
ADF connects attorneys to clients needing pro-bono legal representation to defend their constitutionally protected religious liberties. It also trains newly licensed attorneys how to select and litigate cases.

AMERICAN CENTER FOR LAW AND JUSTICE
www.aclj.org
ACLJ is "specifically dedicated to the ideal that religious freedom and freedom of speech are inalienable, God-given rights" and, when necessary, it litigates to defend these rights.

BECKET FUND
www.becketfund.org
A Washington, D.C.-based public interest law firm that specializes in protecting the free expression of religion, the *Becket Fund* – named after Thomas Becket, the Archbishop of Canterbury who was murdered by Henry II's henchmen – represents members of all religions as equally deserving of protection in a free society.

INSTITUTE FOR JUSTICE
www.ij.org
As the nation's only libertarian public interest law firm, the *Institute for Justice* defends individuals' property, speech, and economic rights through litigation.

LANDMARK LEGAL FOUNDATION
www.landmarklegal.org/DesktopDefault.aspx?tabid=7
Founded in 1976, the foundation is a public interest law firm litigating on behalf of first principles from the American Founding. Specifically, it pursues three accountability projects targeting the liberal federal judiciary, and the illegal activities of the National Education Association, and the Environmental Protection Agency.

LIBERTY COUNSEL
www.lc.org
Liberty Counsel is a "nonprofit litigation, education, and policy organization dedicated to advancing religious freedom, the sanctity of human life, and the traditional family."

PACIFIC LEGAL FOUNDATION
www.community.pacificlegal.org
PLF is a leader in defending property owners' rights, and litigating to stop government over-regulation, especially with farms, private homes, and the environment.

RUTHERFORD INSTITUTE
www.rutherford.org
The Rutherford Institute seeks to provide legal services to people whose religious and civil rights have been violated and to educate the public about threats to constitutional freedom.

THOMAS MORE LAW CENTER
www.thomasmore.org
The Center specializes in defending and promoting "the religious freedom of Christians, time-honored family values, and the sanctity of human life."

Chapter 6

Top Main Stream Media Web Sites

And now for a brief chapter on the "neutral" mainstream media (MSM). Anyone familiar with the establishment news axis knows that objective and unbiased reporting on what's happening gave way a long time ago to so-called opinion journalism in the United States. To read American news from newspapers which openly admit their political affiliation, you need to go to London. Fortunately, DrudgeReport.com links to all major UK papers on its homepage. For the vast majority of US network and cable news, nationally circulated news magazines and newspapers, viewing the world, and the activity within it, has a decidedly progressive slant.

Though their readership and viewership totals are falling, most of the members of the MSM establishment news axis are entrenched enough to still garner attention from bloggers and op-ed writers from the Left and the Right. As long as the proprietors of the new media comment on the opinions of the old media, patriot activists should be aware of what the latter is saying.

No. 1: CNN
www.cnn.com
-see Political Ticker: politicalticker.blogs.cnn.com

No. 2: NEW YORK TIMES
www.nytimes.com
-see The Caucus: thecaucus.blogs.nytimes.com

No. 3: LOS ANGELES TIMES
www.latimes.com
-see Top of the Ticket: latimesblogs.latimes.com

No. 4: FOX NEWS
www.foxnews.com
-see Team Washington: teamwashington.blogs.foxnews.com

No. 5: TIME MAGAZINE
www.time.com/time
-see Swampland: swampland.blogs.time.com

No. 6: ABC NEWS
www.abcnews.go.com
-see Political Punch: blogs.abcnews.com
-see The Note: blogs.abcnews.com/thenote

No. 7: WASHINGTON POST
www.washingtonpost.com
-see Ezra Klein: voices.washingtonpost.com/ezra-klein
-see Chris Cillizza ("The Fix"): voices.washingtonpost.com/thefix

No. 8: CBS NEWS
www.cbsnews.com
-see Public Eye: www.cbsnews.com/sections/publiceye/main500486.shtml

No. 9: MSNBC
www.msnbc.msn.com
-see First Read: firstread.msnbc.msn.com

No. 10: NEWSWEEK
www.newsweek.com
-see The Gaggle: blog.newsweek.com/blogs/thegaggle/default.aspx

Chapter 7

Top Progressive Websites & Blogs Ranked by Popularity (Know Thy Enemy)

In this chapter is a list of the top progressive websites and blogs as ranked by US traffic and the number of unique monthly visitors. The * appearing after many of the publications indicates that visitors to the website can post comments to articles and/or blog posts.

Here's the strategy: when reading content from one of these websites, think of a comment you could post afterwards! Just be honest. Share your views about freedom.

This is important for two reasons.

First, because leaving a conservative or libertarian comment to a progressive article or blog – especially if other patriots do so as well – will alert the webmaster and editors of the site that their active readership may be less progressive than they thought. If enough patriots come to dominate the comments section, the editors may sense a need to moderate or change the tone of their publications.

Second, many "Main Stream Media" reporters scan the comments sections of prominent blogs in order to determine what "the people" are thinking about an issue or person, and then report their findings as news in their newspapers. What they read affects their thinking too. And most main stream reporters read mostly progressive sites and blogs. We The People need to make our opinions known.

TOP FIVE PROGRESSIVE WEBSITES

No. 1: THE HUFFINGTON POST*
www.huffingtonpost.com
The brainchild of socialite and former Republican Arianna Huffington, "HuffPo" is distinguished from other progressive blogs because it features celebrity bloggers from the political and entertainment worlds.

No. 2: SLATE*
www.slate.com
A general-interest publication of The Washington Post Company, Slate is an online news magazine with a strong progressive voice in its content.

No. 3: SALON*
www.salon.com
Located in San Francisco, CA, Salon is a self-described "smart tabloid" that covers politics, news, and entertainment from a progressive perspective.

No. 4: MOVEON.org
www.moveon.org
An online-based political action committee and progressive advocacy organization, Moveon.org was originally founded in response to the impeachment of President Bill Clinton. Since then it has become a staple in the "perpetual campaign" for progressive causes, and served as a main organization and funding source for Democratic campaigns.

No. 5: THE DAILY KOS*
www.dailykos.com
This site is an online progressive coffee house where elected leaders and ordinary citizens discuss the politics of the day from a very progressive perspective.

OTHER IMPORTANT PROGRESSIVE WEBSITES

ACT BLUE*
www.actblue.com
Primarily an online fundraising website supporting "blue state" America, Act Blue also connects Democratic politicians and candidates to progressive activists and donors. Visitors can post comments to the website's blog entries.

AMERICA BLOG*
www.americablog.com
A reliably progressive font of viewpoints on US politics, gay rights, and the Iraq War places this website to the left of many mainstream outlets.

THE AMERICAN PROSPECT
www.prospect.org
The online supplement to a monthly print publication by the same name, TAP covers politics and public policy and promotes itself as a storehouse of "progressive ideas, committed to a just society, an enriched democracy, and effective progressive politics".

COMMON DREAMS*
www.commondreams.org
This website mixes news and opinions from a progressive viewpoint with tools for community organizing and internet activism.

CROOKS AND LIARS*
www.crooksandliars.com
A pioneer in video blogs ("vlogs"), C&L produces progressive news and opinion commentary, along with archives of political events, television, and radio. It also creates its own audio-visual content.

THE DAILY BEAST
www.thedailybeast.com
This website provides a mix of commentary about politics, fashion, and entertainment.

DAILY DISH
www.andrewsullivan.theatlantic.com
A diary-like blog for one-time conservative, current progressive gay activist Andrew Sullivan. Many of his blog posts are linked to by conservatives who criticize his analysis of issues ranging from health care to Sarah Palin.

FIRE DOG LAKE*
www.firedoglake.com
Founded and sourced by former film producers, FDL rose to prominence during the Valerie Plame-Scooter Libby affair. Its writers contribute to other progressive online publications like Huffington Post and Salon.

FIVE THIRTY EIGHT*
www.fivethirtyeight.com
Taking its name from the number of electors in the Electoral College, Five Thirty Eight is primarily a polling aggregation website with a progressive leaning blog.

MEDIA MATTERS*
www.mediamatters.org
A self-described "progressive research and information center" dedicated to combating alleged conservative media bias and misinformation.

MOTHER JONES*
www.motherjones.com
A daily updated online and bi-monthly print publication that specializes in "investigative, political, and social justice reporting." Typically, Mother Jones is to the left of mainstream media publications like The New York Times.

THE NATION
www.thenation.com
Founded at the beginning of the Reconstruction period following the Civil War in support of the Union North, The Nation now describes itself as "the flagship of the Left." It covers news, political, and cultural issues from a reliably progressive perspective.

THE NEW REPUBLIC*
www.tnr.com
TNR advocates a center-left position on fiscal and economic policy, balanced with progressive stances on social issues and a hawkish perspective towards foreign policy.

OPEN LEFT*
www.openleft.com
Part news and analysis hub, part activist website, Open Left is "dedicated toward building a progressive governing majority in America."

TALKING POINTS MEMO
www.talkingpointsmemo.com
Founded during the 2000 Florida recount of presidential ballots, TPM specializes in breaking news and investigative reporting, as well as commentary and high profile bloggers.

THINK PROGRESS
www.thinkprogress.org
A project of the Center for American Progress (CAP), a progressive think tank (see below), is a *de facto* communications arm of the Obama White House due in large part to the link provided by John Podesta, CAP president and transition team leader for Barack Obama. CAP is heavily funded by George Soros, the uber-rich Wall-Street hedge fund insider who famously brought down the Bank of England and the Malaysian currency through foreign exchange speculation.

Chapter 8

Top Progressive Think Tanks

The purpose of a think tank is to collect like-minded intellectuals and give them the financial resources to publish research that supports a specific ideology. Although most media outlets identify them as progressive, most progressive think tanks self-identify as "liberal", in an attempt to confuse their statist big-government positions with classical liberal values and belief in the natural rights of the individual.

Though they may differ in focus, the unifying principle for progressive think tanks is the belief that government involvement is good generally and should be perfected. Thus, progressive think tanks tend to publish research that either argues for more government involvement in a specific area, or for improved management in areas where government is not delivering as expected.

BROOKINGS INSTITUTION
www.brookings.edu
One of the oldest think tanks in Washington, D.C., The Brookings Institution is left-of-center and specializes in foreign, economic, and defense policy studies.

CENTER FOR AMERICAN PROGRESS
www.americanprogress.org
Founded as a progressive think tank, CAP offers policy and communications support to Democratic politicians. It was the single most influential think tank during the Obama Administration's transition to the White House because many of its affiliated staff members became Obama Administration officials.

CENTER FOR DEFENSE INFORMATION
www.cdi.org
Though founded by a retired Navy Rear Admiral, the group is dedicated strengthening American and international security by promoting multilateral cooperation, reducing reliance on nuclear weapons, and enhancing oversight of defense programs.

CENTER FOR ECONOMIC AND POLICY RESEARCH
www.cepr.net
A much-cited economic and domestic policy think tank focusing on issues like Social Security, and developing economies like Latin America.

CENTER FOR INTERNATIONAL POLICY
www.ciponline.org
As stated on its website, CIP stands for "promoting a foreign policy based on cooperation, demilitarization, and respect for human rights."

CENTER FOR AN URBAN FUTURE
www.nycfuture.org
Located in Manhattan, in New York City, the center focuses on problems facing low-income and working class neighborhoods.

CENTER ON BUDGET AND POLICY PRIORITIES
www.cbpp.org
The center works at the state and federal levels to focus policymakers' attention on issues facing low-income and middle class families and individuals by specifically drawing attention to the short- and long-term impact of proposed budget and tax policies on these groups.

THE CENTURY FOUNDATION
www.tcf.org
The foundation's research focuses on economic inequality, the ageing population, preserving civil liberties while combating terrorism, and moving America to a more cooperative role in resolving global problems.

COMMONWEAL INSTITUTE
www.commonwealinstitute.org
In order to achieve its mission to obtain "governing power", the Commonweal Institute styles itself as an "integrator" to connect, convene, and catalyze other think tanks and intellectuals in the progressive movement.

COUNCIL ON HEMISPHERIC AFFAIRS
www.coha.org
Produces research and commentary on Latin America, with a focus on US foreign policy in relation to Latin America.

DEMOCRATIC LEADERSHIP COUNCIL
www.dlc.org

DLC promotes Democratic centrist ideas and policies for the purpose of creating a permanent Democratic majority.

DEMOS
www.demos.org
Demos is a research and activist organization focusing on creating a more equitable society, inclusive democracy, empowered public sector, and responsible US foreign policy.

DRUM MAJOR INSTITUTE
www.drummajorinstitute.org
The institute's stated goal is to create progressive public policy that strengthens and expands the ever-more squeezed middle class and aspiring middle class.

ECONOMIC POLICY INSTITUTE
www.epi.org
EPI produces economic research and commentary focusing on how public policies affect working families and trade unions.

GLOBAL FINANCIAL INTEGRITY
www.gfip.org
A project of the Center for International Policy, GFI "promotes national and multilateral policies, safeguards, and agreements aimed at curtailing the cross-border flow of illegal money."

INSTITUTE FOR POLICY STUDIES
www.ips-dc.org
Founded in 1963 by former Kennedy Administration aides, the institute's focuses on issues related to promoting peace, justice, and the environment.

JOINT CENTER FOR POLITICAL AND ECONOMIC STUDIES
www.jointcenter.org
Produces research and commentary of interest to communities of color, especially black Americans.

NEW DEMOCRAT NETWORK
www.ndn.org
Since splitting with the Democratic Leadership Council, the NDN seeks to promote centrist Democratic candidates and ideas.

NATIONAL SECURITY NETWORK
www.nsnetwork.org
NSN is a left-leaning foreign policy organization that seeks to enhance the Democratic Party's ownership of national security issues.

PROGRESSIVE POLICY INSTITUTE
www.ppionline.org
PPI is a think tank that produces research and commentary for "pragmatic progressives." It is affiliated with the Democratic Leadership Council.

ROOSEVELT INSTITUTION
www.rooseveltinstitution.org
Founded after the 2004 presidential election, the Roosevelt Institution seeks to connect progressive college students through collaborative publications, research, and conferences.

WORLD RESOURCES INSTITUTE
www.wri.org
WRI is an environmental policy think tank that looks for ways to promote sustainable practices in government, industry, and the free market.

About the Authors

Terry Easton is an entrepreneur, economist, and enthusiastic university professor who writes about economics and political affairs. A former trustee of the Center for Libertarian Studies, he is a proponent of the Austrian School of economics as espoused by Ludwig von Mises, Friedrich Hayek, Henry Hazlett, and Murray Rothbard. He rejects the failed ideas of John Maynard Keynes, fiat currency and deficit spending. His previous book, *Stark Raving Mad*, is a collection of the best of his Human Events articles from 2007 through 2009. An optimist on the long-term future, he is passionate about technology and entrepreneurship: "The glass isn't half-full, it's overflowing!"

Ashton Ellis is a writer living in Southern California with graduate degrees in public policy and law. At heart, he is a communicator with experience working as a policy analyst, speech writer, blogger, columnist, and university professor. With *Refounding America*, he hopes to help reestablish the connection between modern public policy and the Founders' philosophy of limited, effective government. Armed with commonsense and a bit of humor, he believes that everyday Americans will reclaim their country with the character necessary to preserve the blessings of life, liberty, and the pursuit of *true* happiness.

Acknowledgements

Terry Easton: First, last and always to Susan, the poet and clown and lover of people big and small; closer to the angels than we know. Thanks to Burt Blumert (we sure miss you), and Gary North and Jack Williams and Harry Browne (who's humming Wagner somewhere), and Bob Kephart (that's 'pedantic', my friend). To Lou Carabini, Lew Rockwell, Ken School-land and Mark Skousen, and the countless other libertarians and lovers of freedom who have shared their dreams of a kinder, freer America where the individual once again is king, the government but a servant, and the Constitution is restored to its Founders' blessed vision.

Ashton Ellis: My deepest appreciation is to my wife Lauren – the kind of soul mate every man should have. I love you with all that I am. Thanks to my parents Ronald and Jane; true patriots and exemplary Christians. Special thanks to Jan Himebaugh – a generous friend who made my contributions to this project possible – and to Floyd Brown for getting us off and running. Finally, thank you Terry. Throughout this endeavor you have been a channel of grace for God to bless me. I am eternally grateful for the presence of you and Sue in my life.

Credits

Tea Party Cartoon, Introduction, copyright by Eric Allie.
Nope Cartoon, Part I, copyright by Nate Beeler.
Octopus Cartoon, Part I, Chapter 3, copyright by Eric Allie.
Talking the Talk Cartoon, Part II, copyright by Nate Beeler.
Tea Bag Tossing Cartoon, Part III, copyright by Nate Beeler.
Tapping the 2010 Elections Cartoon, Part IV, copyright by Dave Granlund.
Economy Worsens Cartoon, Part V, copyright by Mike Lester.
Above cartoons used with permission, provided by: *PoliticalCartoons.com*
US Debt Clock, Part II, Chapter 2, courtesy of *USDebtClock.org*
It's the Sun, Stupid, Part II, Chapter 13, courtesy of *ThePeople'sCube.com*